# Marginalized
## by
## Mark A. Cornelius

ISBN 9781723957413
Kindle Direct Publishing

## QUOTES FROM THE MARGINALIZED

### OUTSIDE OF MY BOX:

Mark invites us into a real, honest conversation and self-exploration about an issue that is centuries old but still plagues us as a society today. *Marginalized* motivated me to look at "my box" where I want to put those I'm comfortable with and then push out all others. I quickly realized that my box is too small and this limits my ability to share the love of Christ. In a day where, as a society we quickly substitute virtual or contractual relationships, Mark calls us to consider living in covenantal relationships with all those around us and especially with our one true God!

—Susan Cress, Spirit Mind Field Specialist YMCA OF MIDDLE TENNESSEE

### A SPECIAL TALENT:

As a student of life, Mark A. Cornelius sees how easy it is for us to formulate opinions, find others with similar notions, and then harden our collective ideas into a scheme. The scheme becomes prejudice, supports our sense of community, and allows us to marginalize those not following the path of our mindset.

As a writer, Mark can take on the tangled association between spiritualism and humanism in a mature and humble style that appeal to both those readers preferring an ideal, mind-conscious approach to reality, as well as to those leaning hard toward a practical, everyday-life experience. Mark has a way of presenting his thoughts as adventures, guiding us on the journey and allowing us to make discoveries for ourselves along the way.

—Paul Uhrig – Book Review America

### THE DEEPER LOOK:

Not only a good look into the meaning of marginalization, but makes you look into your own inner self. *Marginalized* is an informative read and a look into why we treat others the way we do, and why what we see to be helpful is not always the best answer.

—Mark Mitchel – Astro Publishing Review

# FOREWORD

## *The Rev. Sam Clarke*

We live in a world torn apart by division and strife. Groups of people are marginalized from each other over a whole variety of issues. Gender, ethnic background, ideology, world view, and a myriad of other factors make for a divided and often contentious world. At times this division has been tempered by an overriding factor that creates a sense of unity. For example: The United States is a melting pot of ethnic groups, often marginalized from each other by their backgrounds, but who share a common loyalty to their country. Historically they see themselves as Americans first and then whatever ethnic affiliation they share. Sadly, this paradigm has undergone a transformation since the 1960's that has created a very divided nation.

Since the fall of man in the Garden of Eden, history demonstrates that humanity is incapable of sustaining any system of unity for a prolonged period. As a result, conflicts, divisions, wars, etcetera are inherent between individuals and groups marginalized by some factor. Therefore a society requires a system of agreed upon norms or standards (laws) to help alleviate potential conflicts.

Mark insightfully explores the dynamics of human marginalization to help us all better understand their impact on us as individuals and as members of groups. We are all marginalized in the context of the broader human community and we all marginalize others in this same context. For the most part, we tend not to be concerned about marginalizing others or being marginalized. At the same time there are times when marginalization results in significant conflict.

Besides a set of norms to help maintain peace in a culture made up of different individual and groups, there are ways for these individuals and groups to coexist and even work together to overcome whatever else may divide or separate them. One of the most common is a contract. A written agreement to insure both parties live up to the stipulations laid out in the contract. This helps the individuals/groups function together but it does not resolve non-contractual sources of division or conflict.

The question then becomes, *is there a way of creating a harmonious, peaceful relationship between individuals or groups separated by sometimes serious, seemingly insurmountable differences?* The answer is an emphatic "yes", and it is found in understanding the nature of a biblical covenant.

I invite you to join Mark in an in-depth exploration of the issue of human marginalization and how it can be overcome through entering a biblical covenant; particularly the covenant cut between Almighty God and His creation through His Son, Jesus the Messiah.

*This book is dedicated to all who labor and are heavy laden…*
*—each of us, all of us.*

## INTRODUCTION

OVER THE YEARS, as a business person, traveler and student of life, I've witnessed and experienced many cross-sections of life. Humankind's diversity across the planet is amazing but I have also seen that we continue to struggle with our commonality. Why are we so divided into cultures, belief systems, identities and classes?

What is the cause of our pride, our individual drive to segment ourselves from others? When we want to celebrate our uniqueness, words like *individualistic, exclusive, outstanding* and *singular* are used. But when our eccentric natures cause harm, isolation or discord to others, words like *narcissistic, egomaniacal* and *self-centered* enter in.

What makes one person be seen as harmlessly uncommon to others in a good way and what causes another with similar traits to be labeled as pariah? Could it be that the person's behavior might be seen differently depending on the culture and times in which they exist? And why is our tendency to isolate and separate that person, rather than attempt to seek inclusiveness?

Is there really any significant glue, other than our physical DNA that holds us together? In researching this book, I discovered one common thread among us. Each and every one feels a sense of un-belonging that has influenced a portion or all of our lives. Each of us strives to be different, but mourn at the brand it burns into our social self-consciousness.

As a first grader, I remember trying hard to fit in. I was small and not the most savvy socialite. On the other hand, I wanted to somehow stand out in some heroic way; not as an outcast. How to find harmony between the two-acclimation and distinction? The scales never remained balanced. Each of us at some moment in our lives, have become victims of the sting that comes with stigma. And so somewhere within, we have developed a defense mechanism to deal with it. Hungry to be recognized as acceptable, we have learned to separate others, categorizing them into lessor beings than ourselves. This is a painful admission because on the social surface we all want things to look equal. Amazingly, we have found ways of displaying pretended empathy, while in fact implementing conscientiously acceptable methods of enslavement upon those we perceive as less than adequate in the scheme of human society.

Do we convince ourselves that we want the best for others...as long as I, the individual have better? Our isolation tactics may be blatant. Humankind has polished the societal methods we have created to position ourselves above one another in belief and social status, into fine gems, subtle and sublime. We have become clannish masters at defining cultural norms and equally as skilled at stacking the deck against those who do not match

7

our sense of values; those who think and act even slightly differently from ourselves—the *marginalized.*

This book is an exploration of both the marginalized and the *marginalizers.* What distinguishes one from the other, what impact marginalization has had on us socially, and spiritually? And most important, what can be done to unify…is d*e-marginalization* even something we honestly want to strive for, and if so how can we seek community with those who we think to be "not quite up to snuff"?

As I develop the idea of our *marginalization mindset,* other strange words and concepts are used in new context, *slanged* to help clarify this radical paradigm: Words such as *covenant, midrash and echad.* My hope is to shine a light on the nearly invisible cultural constraints we have set forth and by revealing their affects, help through awareness to begin reversing their effects. This will require some dialogue and paradigm shifting, but I'm up for it if you are. To that end, throughout the book, you will see headings marked WAIT A MINUTE. In these moments, I'll present some radical discoveries, things we are doing either intentionally or subconsciously to perpetuate a state of marginalization.

Whether or not you agree with my premise, I'm anxious to get your reactions to these insights, hoping they will energize a whole new discussion about the great need to become more aware of, address and explore alternatives to our marginalization tendencies. You can reach out to me at www.MarkCornelius.me and I will do as best I can not to marginalize you.

Sincerely,

Mark A. Cornelius

**Preliminary note:** All Bible passages quoted come from the English Standard Version unless otherwise indicated.

*But God chose the foolish things of the world to shame the wise; God chose the weak things of the world to shame the strong. God chose the lowly thing of this world and the despised things…so that no one may boast before Him.*

—Paul of Tarsus, 1<sup>st</sup> letter to the Corinthians

# CONTENTS

## CHAPTER ONE—GETTING TO KNOW ME

*Who causes sadness, among the gladness, what makes us cry?*
*What is the reason, for friends who leave us—it drains my laughter dry.*
*Where do I fit in, where do I belong?*
*Thought I had it all, thought the price was paid,*
*But here I am alone again.*
*Where do I fit in, where do I belong?*
*I didn't get back what love I gave—I'm just water down the drain.*

—Mark A. Cornelius
Lyrics-Where Do I Belong

I HAVE TO ADMIT, until recently I've not given great thought toward our natural tendency of separating rather than integrating. After all, I live close to Nashville. That's right, I reside just south of Music City, in Franklin, Tennessee, smack dab in the center of Williamson County, the 7th wealthiest county in the United States. Our median income is right at $100,000 per year, and 95% of us have a high school education or above. We have a healthy mix of races and minimal racial conflict. We all seem to have nice cars and houses. Our population poverty rate is nearly absent at 5.2%, our unemployment rate is even more impressive at 3.7%. We are, to put it mildly, well off. There is economic growth, comfort, beautiful countryside, jobs for anyone who wants one and a community of people who like to "get along" in the way all Southerners in the United States like to get along. No one wants trouble here; everyone is friendly toward one another. That's just the way we do things in Williamson County. That's just the way it looks and feels. So, all of us in Williamson County and its surrounding region should be very, very happy and feel very well served…shouldn't we? After all, it doesn't get much better than here.

Yet, there are some other statistics hinting that maybe what I just bragged about is not quite accurate.
The Tennessee Department of Health reported that in 2014, 25 people died from drug overdoses in Williamson County.[1] That doesn't sound like a lot in the bigger picture, but that was an increase from 19 the year before and, for our little community, one is too many. Rapes and violent crimes are also on the rise. Just up the street in Nashville, the rate of violent crime has been on a steady increase, rising 8.6% including 17,250 murders in 2016.[2] Suicides? Oh yes, we have those too although every resource I hunted down seemed to convolute the actual number by comparing it only as a lower percentage to that of our neighbor to the north, Nashville. As best as I can figure it, our suicide rate is also sadly increasing, currently recorded at 1375 people in 2017.[3] There is even a bridge nestled in our beautiful countryside that is notorious for attracting people from all over the county to come in quest of ending their lives. The Williamson County Sheriff's Department records show tragically, at least 15 attempted suicides at the bridge from 2005 to 2017.

Statistics and reports are one thing, but what they don't measure is the struggle of those who live on the bottom rungs of the ladder; the lower income earners who work in, but are not able to live in the affluent areas. They may drive more than an hour each way to get to their daily jobs. They may live in beautiful rural countryside, but there lurks bigger problems. Western and southern Williamson County it seems is a hotspot for opioid traffic. It is also notorious for harboring one of the highest illegal meth-lab rates in the

---

[1] https://www.neighborhoodscout.com/tn/franklin/crime
[2] https://patch.com/tennessee/nashville/violent-crime-tennessee-rose-2016-compared-previous-year-fbi
[3] https://franklinhomepage.com/2018-state-of-suicide-report-shows-4-increase-year-over-year/

country.[4] The infant abandonment, abortion and partner abuse rate is soaring and every day, we hear more unusual stories of sex-trafficking, including a recent sting leading to the indictment of 22 men seeking to have sex with minors.[5]

This book is not intended to be an analytical numbers dump—I want these facts to become part of a heartfelt mutual exploration, not a head-banging-question. So, from the heart—how can this be? How can a perfect place of panacea harbor a great cancer, a sore that either goes ignored or that we just won't believe to be real?

We hear about these things happening, shake our heads and perhaps offer a prayer. Maybe we even donate to some governmental/social-service or faith-based group that assists with public awareness, legal enforcement, counseling or provisions to the victims. We feel better and then move on, enjoying our daily comforts until the next tragic news of abuse or calamity brings up the toughest question of all…

### —We are looking better, but are we actually getting better?

We are very good at masking the very issue of marginalization: manufacturing charts and graphs, blasting and posting socially conscious blogs, loudly expressing opposing opinions. We claim better understanding from one group verses another and sterilize the dilemma called marginalization through our analytic discourse. Can we find a way to personalize the problem?

If you're willing to take a stab at "sticking with it" for a while, I invite you to join me in an exercise…right now. For starters, from this chapter forward, I'm going to be addressing you as "you" and would ask that you return the favor. Strange, I know. We're not in some room together or anything like that. But if you have a reaction to what I say, positive or negative, go ahead and actually speak it out. It will start us on a path of discussion that will seem more intimate. I hope that we can flex our "agreement and disagreement muscles" a bit and by some methods that will be suggested later, learn how to trust our common ground rather than abandon any hope of progression in the relationship of humankind.

---

[4] This is a difficult statistic to track—an embarrassing one for our well-to-do population to advertise. Read https://www.thefix.com/content/tennessee-no1-meth-pseudoephedrine91462
[5] https://www.tennessean.com/story/news/local/williamson/brentwood/2017/11/09/tbi-announces-significant-human-trafficking-sting-brentwood-22-indicted-brentwood-human-trafficking/848135001/

**WAIT A MINUTE...**

—where's the fun in that? It's much more satisfying to throw rocks of reasoning at our opponents, isn't it? But maybe, just maybe, if we can somehow find a way to connect with those we marginalize, and recognize our own self-inflicted marginalization, then we won't be so prone to cast aside others in our future together.

**DEFINING OUR REAL PROBLEM**

A popular term for it today is *disenfranchising* which suggests enslavement, domination and oppression of another. There are plenty of media blitzes about this; who's doing the enslaving and who's being enslaved or abused—everyone has an opinion on it—all of these reports and sentiments can be included in a broader definition that I call *marginalization*. It's a concept with origins rooted throughout the fabric of human history.

The term recently came to my mind during a conversation with a friend who pastors a local church. We were talking about the community that the congregation served and how appearances suggested that our town was strongly unified in faith and services, both to the well-fit and to the downtrodden within our reach.

Both my friend and I recognized that this appearance was extremely deceptive, that there were many pockets of "unwelcomed" people. By lifestyle, events, economic condition, health or racial history (either through choice or circumstance), *the marginalized* have been shunted off. We, the community at large, and yes, our church, had even encouraged them into corners of convenience, so that we and they would not have to engage in the difficult conversation of our differences. We had excused them away as not-able or not-caring to fit in to the community norm.

**WAIT A MINUTE...**

—If true, if the coined condition "marginalized" exists on a pandemic scale, then shouldn't we be alarmed? Shouldn't we be taking action to cure the ill? And if our action is not that shocking to us: why not? Why are we so accepting of the situation? What has caused us to become so acceptably distanced and calloused toward our fellow brothers and sisters on the planet? If our marginalizing <u>is</u> truly recognized as a faulty condition, what can be done about it? No, let's make this more personal: What can I do about it? What can you and I do about it?

## THE MARGINALIZED IN REAL-TIME

Throughout this book, I'd like to share some true stories of marginalization in hopes that you might relate on a personal level with the reality of being marginalized. The examples are "real-life", but I don't want to point fingers in fault (there are likely well deserved fingers pointing my way as well). Therefore, the *tellings* will leave out real names and will be generalized enough that (I hope) the message gets across without unnecessary embarrassment. I'll start with a story about one marginalized man's needs.

The man, whom I'll call Frank, had to return to the city where he had had a bad string of circumstances. He was admittedly responsible for much of his misfortune and ended up having to deliver some papers and penalty money to the municipal government in order to get his commercial driver's license reinstated. Frank had left the city to avoid a myriad of personal conflicts, but eventually made up his mind that it was time to get his life back together. His return journey required a cross-country trip which included hitching a ride with a trucker who was able to drop him off within 20 miles of his intended destination. Determined, Frank began walking the rest of the way, hauling his large backpack up a main road into town on a very warm Sunday morning.

As he was passing a church, a couple who were just arriving for service, stopped their car beside the hiker and asked if he had far to go. He explained his objective and the couple offered to take him the rest of the way. There was only one catch. They wanted to first attend worship and so they asked if Frank wanted to join them.

Frank had heard the gospel preached, but had always avoided the commitment of faith. This day though, he felt compelled, whether by the opportunity not to miss a good ride into town, or by the friendly invitation, and agreed to share the moment.

The hiker parked his backpack, which contained all his worldly possessions, in the couple's car. They then walked into the building together. As their guest apologized for his appearance, the couple assured him that he would be welcomed, should not feel out of place and that this group was a very "casual" congregation. They appeared confident that there would be a great "reaching out" to Frank.

When they began introducing the traveling man, their Sunday friends seemed polite and conversational, but the only people who seemed to want to sit and learn more about Frank's story in depth was the couple whom had first reached out to him. They led him into the sanctuary and sat alongside him for the service.

The traveler asked if he could borrow some paper to take notes during the sermon, which he did. He borrowed a Bible and the couple guided him toward the scriptures that were being referenced. Frank had good reading skills and followed along silently.

After the sermon, the pastor asked for discussion and reaction to his topic. It was then that the couple stood up and once more introduced Frank as a visitor, so that everyone in the congregation would be aware of this soul in need. The couple explained the circumstances of their encounter with Frank and then asked him if he had anything to say. He did indeed.

Frank had remembered what the sermon was about, even referring to his notes and sharing how the message had impacted him. He thanked everyone for their hospitality and then said something extraordinary, "I appreciate all that y'all have done for me and I can see Jesus here. I want to believe in him."

## WAIT A MINUTE...

—What had just happened? Did the Spirit just enter this man's heart and did he just confess faith? The couple became excited and asked him, in front of the fellowship, if he would reaffirm his belief. He did! He also asked for prayer to accomplish his goal of getting his life back together. The couple invited the others in the room to gather around this new man to pray for him and offer hands of support be laid on him. The pastor vocalized the prayers of these people in thanks to God for the work of the Spirit.

One would have expected the brothers and sisters in Christ to jump into a whooping celebration. Instead, after the prayers, the pastor announced, "Amen, praise God," and moved on to the next person's comments about the sermon subject. In other words, "Thanks, next topic matter."

Since that time, Frank continues to be encouraged by the inviting couple. They helped him with supplies, finding a job and supported him as much as possible for his life and spiritual goals. He did get his commercial license back and in fact now drives a semi-truck cross country, sharing the hope of the gospel to others he encounters on his journey.

As for the congregation? To my knowledge, not one person, beside the noted couple has asked after Frank. To them, at least in outward appearance, he remains a memory, marginalized into the ranks of the body of Christ.

Please understand in hearing this story. I don't want to disparage church groups or faith groups or any group for that matter. This is not a tale about the failure of religion, but rather a testimony to the common behavior of humankind. To me this is one of many examples of how we as a world-culture are prone to push away…casually dismiss…those who do not measure up to our standards. It may not be that we wish ill on others; more likely it is that we just want them to stay in the small corner of life to which we imagine they belong. They can succeed and grow all they want; we will even provide money and goods to help them do so; as long as they do it marginalized, quietly and separately, outside of the view of our comfortable cabins. Or, there is the even less-attractive consideration: Are we just so busy accomplishing our agendas and schedules, that anything, anyone outside of our purpose driven lives, do not matter?

Why aren't we taking time to see, hear and respond to tragedies and needs happening all around us? How have we become so self-focused?

## WHY DO WE MARGINALIZE?

For myself, in order to find answers to this compelling issue I had to first get a better handle on understanding the verb from which my neologism evolved. According to Mr. Webster, there is a very negative slant to the verb:

> **marginalize**
> *v.* —to relegate (see RELEGATE 2) to an unimportant or powerless position within a society or group[6]

I was OK with this interpretation until I realized that, in the case of my own marginalization, I had freely chosen my segregation.

## WAIT A MINUTE…

—My apologies to you, I neglected to point out that there is another nuance to marginalization. We can, and do, self-marginalize. How do I support such a bizarre hypothesis? Easily, the support comes from deeply rooted personal experience.

---

[6] https://www.merriam-webster.com/dictionary/Marginalize?src=search-dict-hed

## MARGINALIZATION IN REAL-TIME

When I was in High School, I joined the choir. Our choral director offered an ambitious goal of a two week singing tour in Europe. We raised funds as a group, planned and practiced as a group and became familiar with one another in the way that any mission-minded organization coalesces. But as with all associations, the individuals bring to the table some very private issues that can affect the entire batch. I was no exception.

I had just started exploring my adolescence. I was experiencing the emotional roller coaster known as dating and was also wading the waters of my newly found faith in God. In a word, I was zealous (some people from my past have said, annoyingly so) in my turn from atheist to worshiper. Honestly, although not unpopular, I felt a personal estrangement, observing other's practices and not feeling a sense of belonging, except to the "bigger cause" of the tour.

So, when we arrived in the foreign land, I felt doubly removed, both from my traveling companions and from the very different world into which we had been planted. Though I admit at the time I had pangs of loneliness, I also felt a true sense of freedom; being able to make of this adventure, whatever I wanted. I began watching and listening, asking questions (as best I could, considering the language barrier), writing down my observations and learning/integrating my discoveries into my newly developing spiritual mindset and worldview.

Though feeling apart, I also realized I desperately wanted to walk alongside others who might share my epiphanies. But when I tried to share my thoughts and observation, the rest of the crew seemed disinterested. Hence I continued as a loner, assimilating and logging my exploits for future reflection.

Over the years, looking back on that moment, I've come to recognize that my teen pilgrimage was the beginning of my love for penning the written word. I also now see the vast blessings it prepared in me. One evident example is how I have come to discern social nuances and filter my worldview of current events through historical and spiritual contexts. Though still not absolutely perfected, I strive to listen and watch prior to opening my heart and soul to others. And that requires a strange method—*self-imposed marginalization.*

So, to me, being set apart is not always bad. I like my exclusive club status and obviously argue that I am NOT powerless over my relegation. Am I alone in this approach? Am I missing something? I submit that many, if not all of us through the ages on this planet, have at least occasionally chosen a path of seclusion in order to evaluate new environments we are about to enter into.

Therein lays the danger. Knowing our own personal tendencies, we are likely to project them onto others, assuming (or justifying) that, at the particular time we are casting another soul aside, that they "probably" are grateful for our (my) avoidance in seeking deeper relationship. Thus, we have become a world of ships passing in the night, seldom attempting to engage one another at levels that are life, spirit and world changing.

And so, for the purpose of sticking to the main point of this book, I'd like to begin with the assumption that we will all at times self-impose marginalization on ourselves—our individual choice, our consequences, possibly good, possibly bad. That being said, most forms of marginalization are outwardly directed and therefore unhealthy and unproductive. If you disagree, there's a simple solution…close the book and…marginalize me. Don't worry, I'll survive, but regretfully, you and I won't have the opportunity for shaping our opinions together by honest, truly open-minded exploration.[7] I would be honored to have you walk with me on this journey, and even more honored to discover together, concepts lost to society which may very well save us from marginalizing one another into non-existence.

---

[7] In the next chapter, I'm going to offer up a name for, and put some meat on the bones of this debate technique. If you opt out now, you'll be missing a great concept discussion. But, it's up to you. If this is the last page you read, so long and I hope to see you again soon!

## CHAPTER TWO—GETTING TO KNOW YOU

*From the errors of others, a wise man corrects his own.*
—Publilius Syrus. Syrian writer 85–43 BC

I'D LIKE TO SUGGEST WE *MIDRASH* A[8] BIT, but you may be like a lot of folks I know in my neck of the woods. You see, in good old Williamson County, Tennessee, midrash is not the preferred form of discourse. And there is that other little thing—most folks have no clue what midrash is. That little thing can be fixed right now:

Midrash is a very old Hebrew[9] term merging the meaning of both *explanation* and *debate*. It is both a form of teaching and a method of argument where the teacher questions the student into understanding. Midrash is, in my opinion, the most effective of learning tools, but it requires something few of us have today…patience. It also requires a great risk of exposure—the misrashing parties gaining a deeper and more valued understanding of one another. Midrash typically assumes disagreement—a form of chaos: *Ra-ah*—from the parties in debate, and strives to bring about agreement—a form of unity and peace: *Echad, Shalom.*

And so appears the proverbial hiccup. By *misdrashing* with someone, I might offend them by challenging their ideals, beliefs and worldview. I might cause them to become defensive by interrupting their quest for comfortability[10]. After all, we all want to be comfortable, right? Last but not least, in offending them, I might cause them to rethink their position, possibly infecting them with new ideas. Worst of all, they might infect me with their ideas and then we might have to seek out a whole new belief paradigm together; in which we can coexist in harmony with common beliefs. Who knows: By midrashing, we might actually find a near perfect agreement abandoning all our petty disagreements. Of course none of what I just proposed is possible—the approach suggested would be considered uncivil in today's world of erroneously defined tolerance. We as a species are simply not capable of such bonding…

—or are we?

---

[8] This is the term I teased about in Chapter One: Thanks for hanging in there. Midrash is a Jewish transliterated noun: midrash—an interpretive act, seeking the answers to religious questions. https://www.myjewishlearning.com/article/midrash-101/. I have taken the liberty however to use a more ancient Hebraic approach; employing every word as a working verb. Hence, *to midrash*—an act of dialogue to discover unified agreement.

[9] I'm just letting you know right up front. I'm not Jewish by lineage. I just love this stuff and the people through whom it was inspired.

[10] Comfortability should not be confused with peace. They are different and we'll *midrash* on that subject later.

At the risk of offending you (I apologize in advance), here's a few beliefs of mine I'll share with you.

By my research:

> A). I don't think we have evolved into some new improved state of civility at all, and…

> B). I do think we have chosen to nurture a reoccurring problem in our shared psyches—We <u>want</u> to marginalize one another and we seek ways to do just that, even with our closest family, friends and neighbors.

In order to prove the point, I need to run through some history with you. Please bear with me; I'll do my best to make this entertaining.

## THE PRIMORDIAL PROBLEM

All you have to do is read the legends and writings of old to see the unfolding of marginalization and its consequences. As an example, let's go to the example that has become the most controversial, yet historically accurate of all. Even if one considers the book of Genesis only as a metaphorical accounting, it effectively demonstrates our historical tendencies and laser-points the persisting problem. Paraphrasing:

> In chapter three, Adam and Eve hide themselves from God, because they have new ideas that don't jive with His. In chapter four, Cain marginalizes Able to the extreme, for, of all things acting out a more well received approach in worship.

> Genesis chapter six doesn't mention much outright about Noah's segregation from society, but the rendering does suggest that he and his family, being righteous, and humankind being corrupt, would not have been compatible neighbors. In the end…that end, the marginalizing occurred on a supernatural level and so the cultural conflict of that time seemed to become moot.

Even if I were to ignore the Biblical rendering of things, it's very obvious, proven throughout various ancestral records and civil histories, that men and women from all walks have consistently demonstrated very selfish agendas. From our start, marginalization was one of the most serious challenges with which the human race would have to struggle. There appears to have been, and continues to be, an unnatural component in the soul of humankind for dissecting ourselves into separate clans rather than weaving ourselves into one common social unit.

The Mesopotamian, Babylonian and Egyptian kingdoms? Roman Greco conquests, the Kahns—Genghis and Kublai? The Cast System of India , the Roman Catholic Church, Christian Reformists, the Shoguns of Asia? The English, French, Dutch, Portuguese and Spanish empires of Europe, Islamic Caliphates? The New World as it continues to unfold; Imperialism, Progressivism, Religious Separatism, Darwinism, Capitalism, Socialism, Communism, Nationalism? Manifest Destiny? The New Deal, the Great Society, the New World Order? Need I go on? All sound grand and power-filled…

Societies rise and fall to this day dictating who should serve, who should be served, and who should be pushed off to the side. A hierarchy formed almost immediately: the strong over the weak; the opportunist subjugating the unfortunate. Our choices sometimes made by the individual; sometimes by superiors on behalf of, or at the expense of the individual, depend on the needs of the *hierarchy d'jour*.

Please don't get me wrong, most of these dynasties have suggested beginnings in well-intentioned societal management. All of them took it upon themselves to define the acceptable and the unacceptable. Each one of these formed around a select group who enjoyed increasing comfort and security with each marginalizing conquest.

There has always been a struggle within societies for superiority. Who is best to lead? What authority do they possess that marks them as leaders? And then, there are the others…those, supposedly subservient to the ones who hold the big stick. How did they become "lesser"…marginalized…to the supposedly "greater"?

### THE MARGINALIZED IN REAL-TIME

A constant battle remains evident, surviving the eons—those who have power trying to keep it while those who are outside of the power-grid wrestle to obtain better footing. But what if there is more to it than a simple quest for dominance?

Here's another story for you that sheds light on how some of us have used marginalization to gain status and advantage over others.

> Coming out of the dark ages, the kingdom of France evolved into a feudal system of loosely held fiefdoms ruled by the king and queen. The cost of maintaining the kingdom and keeping the peace was supported through taxes. A political battle ensued as to who received the highest benefit and if that privileged group was responsible for paying more for those privileges. During this same time, wars and changing alliances necessitated that the king grant "favors" to those who supplied

manpower, resources and funding to the kingdom's causes. Advancing at this same time, a merchant class (the *Mercantiles*) increased in number and became a tax target due to their rapidly increasing affluence without *title of privilege*. Complicating all of this, the French Catholic Church grew increasingly powerful, demanding homage and even daring to hint that they were the true rulers of the kingdom.

Out of this turmoil, a hierarchy of three *etates*—estates emerged, each obligated to the monarchy to a greater or lesser extent. The first estate was the Clergy, who were bound to protect the Ruling Class under the authority of God. The second estate was the Nobility, those whom the King deemed worthy of reward due to favor or in payment for service. The third estate was the Commoners which included the Merchantiles. This third class, particularly the Merchantiles bore the brunt of financial costs in supporting the kingdom. This socio-political marginalization shut off the influencing voices of those who were burdened with the heavy lifting for the kingdom's stabilization, survival and advancement.

Wow, it appears that marginalization has always existed, waiting to be recognized, but coincidentally marginalized as an embarrassing flaw we want swept under the rug. Are we so different now, choosing a path that leads us on a segregated journey, always wondering why even the most socially conscious ones of us sense some inner emptiness or alone-ness—some inherent marginalization?

The same mindset echoes today via the marginalizing elitist's self-appointed immunities and bureaucratic controls; purposefully nurtured to impose penalties and benefits according to the marginalizer's preferences. How is it possible that we allow, even design such unequal prominence into the fabric of our community lives?

**HOW CAN IT BE?**

NOW I HOPE YOU'VE COME TO SUSPECT AS I HAVE, that marginalization is not a new phenomenon. But that raises a whole new question. Are we devolving into something less than our heritage would suggest? Or is our marginalizing tendency *Standard Operating Procedure*—an unavoidable consequence of our inherited hardwiring?

## CHAPTER THREE—GETTING TO KNOW "THEY"

*All differences in this world are of degree, and not of kind,*
*because oneness is the secret of everything.*

—*Swami Vivekananda.*19th-century East-Indian mystic

## THEN THERE WAS MACK

IN DOCTOR SEUSS'S CLASSIC, *YERTLE THE TURTLE*[11], Mack, the lowest of the low in the stack, was not a mover and by no means wanted to be a shaker. He was just trying to do his job. As backbreaking as it was, he was there to serve his purpose. Mack wasn't perceived as <u>that</u> important, He wasn't trying to be <u>that</u> rebellious; he was just another "they", distanced from the deciders and climbers above him. And sadly, being who he was, he was marginalized. More sadly for the other marginalized turtles between Mack and Yertle, the truth of Mack's value was realized too late. And it all had to do with the word apostrophized earlier in this paragraph—*they*.

Now here's a question for the ages—Who are "they"? We, you and I, use the collective possessive "they" to identify a known or unknown conspiracy of members who always seem bent on our enslavement to their way of doing things. Don't deny it. I've heard too many people invoke "they" as a universal curse upon some establishment whose methods cause frustration to our personal or collective objectives.

The trick is that "they" seem to morph and change according to the adversarial circumstances. They could be as small as our family and neighbors or as ominous as governments, countries, secret societies, religious groups, fanatics, terrorist organizations and the like.

I'd like to suggest that, in order to understand how we marginalize is not only accomplished by how we control others' status, but how we impart control to others—how we allow the exploits of "they". Just for the fun of it, let's try to define "they" a little more neatly, putting skin on the bones of the elusive nemesis.

---

[11] Yertle the Turtle, Dr. Seuss, pub. 1958

## MARGINALIZATION SECTORS

If "they" truly exist, then they must have traits that distinguish them. I'll call these, *sectors*. Each sector might be used to define a group or a sect who might marginalize me to their benefit and possibly jeopardize my own welfare. Examples of sectors includes individuals or groups with commonalities such as:

| | |
|---|---|
| **Age** | **Racial Background** |
| **Social Status** | **Lifestyle** |
| **Family/Tribe** | **Local/Territorial Community** |
| **Gender** | **Interpersonal Interests** |
| **Economics** | **Selfish Desire** |
| **Politics** | **Spiritual Orientation** |
| **Ethnics** | |

This is not an inclusive list and the designations can be much more subtle. Also approval by and inclusion in one sector, does not suggest approval by or inclusion in another. The same goes for the disapproval from any sector. Within sectors marginalization can discriminate upwards and downwards. Those accepted as "normal" in society or politics can be easily marginalized within their own circles because of internal hierarchies—how long they have claimed membership, how prominent or vocal they are, etc.
So "they" can either be a group of greater, or lessor quality than we; "they" can be in our group or outside of our group…

> —*"they" could be me, and…*
> —*"they could be you.*


## WAIT A MINUTE…

—am I suggesting that I am "they"…that all of "we" are "they"? If that is true, then we are all marginalizing one another – no matter how high or low we are in Yertle's stack! How? How can I be both marginalized and marginalizer?

Our human nature is complicit. We claim ourselves, "not in control" by blaming some far removed entity for any misfortunes we may experience or that we have caused. How convenient. The blame for marginalization is never ours, it is "theirs".

But if we are "they", if we are all our own greater rival, determining who possess societal privileges; who becomes the relegated? Who are we, that we justify pushing aside lesser beings in favor of our better stronger standard? The dirty little secret is that we all seek to control our immediate and extended environment. True, some of us aspire to control more. A few of us dream to climb to the very top of the heap. Seuss got it right in Yertle:

"All mine!" Yertle cried. "Oh, the things I now rule! / I'm king of a cow! And I'm king of a mule!"

When nations, societies and communities morph between the desires of individual and group interests, there is also a proclivity to seek common direction, regardless of common or individual purpose. In other words,

*I want to act individually, and I want others to act just like me[12]*

The study from which the statement above is derived implies several other important social realities. There is safety in numbers when all agree—don't you agree? Just consider the behavior of most school children, especially those on the cusp of adulthood. They test the system, waiving a rebellious spirit as their banner, all the time making sure there are other very similar rebellious spirits very close by. As soon as they find themselves truly isolated, most students of the counterculture will quickly seek some level of conformity. What happens when this group-think behavior is considered on a broader scale? Would it not alleviate rather than encourage marginalization?

**GROUP MARGINALIZATION PLAYED OUT IN THE WORLD**

WE IN THE DEVELOPED WORLD LIVE IN A NEW AGE OF WONDERS. Science and government have neatly melded into a cooperative that benefits all. Food sources are becoming more plentiful, economics are well balanced with only an occasional interest rate or debt adjustment necessary here or there. Housing, access to comforts and communication are unparalleled. Sure there are still curveballs—the occasional drought, storm and earthquake; the social uprising and unexpected change in political regimes—but overall they even out, and so we, by historical standards, observe ourselves to be better off, evolutionarily upgraded and possibly even privileged.

Yet, there is still poverty and struggle around the globe. Third world countries are still impaired by poor food production, economics, regime change and exploitation. Some would argue though that even those places have seen some improvements.[13] But who of us is truly improved? The convenience and opportunity for comfort of today's world are far beyond any time before—is that all we are about? Is our wellbeing truly about our

---

[12] https://books.google.com/books?hl=en&lr=&id=1fsW-
k5wypkC&oi=fnd&pg=PA157&dq=study+on+individuals+rebellion+and+conformity&ots=X4LfK8XH8_&sig=G1dGK7nRBj1yCjW
CkkAxHQewj-w#v=onepage&q=study%20on%20individuals%20rebellion%20and%20conformity&f=false
[13] https://insights.som.yale.edu/insights/how-has-globalization-benefited-the-poor

individual and communal contentment? Following that line of questioning leads to another more difficult query—When speaking of comfort, what if one of us makes another one of us…uncomfortable? Who, in that circumstance, is considered the true victim?

## THE MARGINALIZED IN REAL-TIME

GREECE 2013: A Romani couple was arrested by the Farsala police for abducting a four year old girl. It seems the dark haired, dark eyed man and woman, were suspected of a crime because the child had blonde hair and blue eyes. A similar event occurred in Ireland the very same week when DNA testing was required to prove two blonde-haired, blue-eyed children were related to dark skinned parents. In each of these cases, the children did prove to be in fact family to the suspects. Apparently the crossing gene traits which caused the suspicions are common among Romanies— – derogatorily recognized by most of the world population as Gypsies.

We think we understand the world around us. We most often mean well when we intervene or kick into prevention-mode.. But many times, we act according to mores that cannot and should not be assumed for all across all cultural boundaries. Based on the historical record, we are often prone to engineer our governments and ethics around provincial beliefs that do well for some, not-so for others. Sometimes the majority is the benefactor, sometimes the minority. Regardless of the victor-marginalizer, a victim-marginalizee is the result.

Please don't get me wrong, criminals who have been justly sentenced fit the marginalized status as well and I'm not saying that we unlock the prison gates. What I do want to emphasize is that we examine our marginalizing behavior in depth, across all strata of our culture to weed out unsound traditions which may be cleaving away populations who want the same thing as we in Williamson County, Tennessee.

"Oh Mark, you're sounding like some kind of activist, wanting to stir the pot," some might say. On the contrary, I hope to keep the pot from being stirred. I would rather see us readily recognize our marginalizing behavior, because in truth, it promotes isolation of people and classes. In isolating, we sheer off the opportunity to dialogue, infuse and…midrash our beliefs.

Why do we do that? What is it that keeps us in marginalizing mode? To answer those questions, we need to look at what appears to be our natural willingness, the barometer we use to decide if a cause is worthy or unworthy of our efforts.

In the current age of moral relativism, our overall global society is…

| Willing to... | Unwilling to... |
| --- | --- |
| —fund programs to help support specific marginalized sectors of societies | —assist in breaking down the community barriers that created the marginalized person/population in the first place |
| —recognize and encourage sectors of marginalized society | —seek ways to de-marginalize encourage sectors of marginalized society, reuniting them , seeking common association |
| —create awareness programs to point out marginalized sectors in need | —enter into neighborhoods, homes and communities to become directly engaged with individuals, groups and families who desire authentic relationships while battling their hardships |
| —report on the great accomplishments that money and assistance programs provide | —follow through with continual relationship-building programs to help eliminate marginalized sectors altogether |

To my eyes, reviewing this *Willingness Chart* seems to indicate that we are only willing to play a hand in starting the process of reconciliation, not in seeing it through to its entirety. And if we're unwilling to walk the entire process through to its conclusion…there will be an alternate, imperfect conclusion.

Yes, everyone who reads this will offer exceptions to the observations, but they are exactly that—exceptions. The proof is even in the advertising of our charitable organizations and well-intentioned hearts. We are assured that our money will be put to good use. We are encouraged as Christians, other faith-based groups and world benefactors to join up for mission work—where we are shepherded for a very short trip to some distant land, neighborhood or social cause, to build a house or school or something. Then we are ferried back to our protective cloisters, all the more grateful that we are not counted among the ranks of "those poor unfortunates".

Am I cynical? I don't believe so; more hopeful that we can recognize what we do and by adjusting our intent ever so slightly, change our desire to rule the marginalized.

**WAIT A MINUTE...**

—did I just imply that we want control over those we set apart? It may be that exactly. It may also be more a factor of controlling the circumstances of our interactions, again to make sure the *influenced* do not unnecessarily impact the *influencers*.

## THE MARGINALIZED IN REAL-TIME

In order to rule over the marginalized, we first need to look at the basic behavioral triggers that drive us to marginalize. A great way to do that is to pick a point in the past and observe a group of folks who were marginalizing very well. By their example we can make an honest comparison to our own marginalizing behavior.

WHEN IN ROME: From its origins, the Roman Empire (not to be confused with the Roman Republic) was masterful at shunting off those who did not fit their model for society. Although senatorial debate was the model set up for resolving issues, it was intended primarily for the purpose of solidifying a plan, not changing minds or direction. So well did this system work for the *Imperium,* its rulers, magistrates and patricians that the Latin word for opposition—*Contra*, is difficult to find in the governmental procedures of the day.

If someone became consistently opposed to a rule or ruler and was too loud or active about it, they were either brought before a tribunal court and offered a trial by magistrate, or they were quietly (in most cases) removed from civic influence. Whether by imprisonment or exile, the opposer was silenced and quietly cast aside without fanfare. These practices appeared to be the model for communities as well as the government and so; little is seen of Roman protest. Instead, more likely was the practice of expanding tolerances.

By the end of the Roman Empire, rules and morals became so vague that essentially, anything was permissible. The marginalized were allowed most behavioral pursuits as long as they were peacefully and invisibly exercised.[14]

Our governmental and community structures are not dissimilar. In fact our rules have evolved more into conveniences in which to hide from unfortunate reality. We offer what we call protection…liberties for anyone who claims victim status, as long as the victimization fits socially acceptable norms. Those who do not fit that mold have a choice; either to find ways to carefully and quietly blend their values and practices into tolerable community routines; or to have their status changed to "outcast". Either way, the power of protest and activism, although heralded today as some great right, is a deception. Only those who embrace the progressively acceptable/popular counter-cultural banners of the day may dissent. All others are persona non grata.

---

[14] https://www.ancient.eu/Roman_Empire/

**REASONS FOR MARGINALIZATION**

But it's not just about how we marginalize, is it? It's about, why? Why would I want to interfere with someone's life-walk? What gives me...any of us... that right? Back to the historical record: from our beginnings, we have allowed emotional and selfish concerns direct our inclusion of others into our fold. Some of those concerns may be healthy, others:

> Envy...
> Frustration...
> Anger...
> Discomfort...
> Willful Desire...
> Greed...
> Fear...
> Woundedness...
> Social Injury...

>         —not so much.

To protect our majority or minority interests, like the Romans, we have become ourselves, a walled-in system of protocols, allowing into our consideration, interactions and protection only those who will behave accordingly. Aren't we clever? We have learned from the Romans, have even advanced our techniques, marginalizing in far more subtle ways. Let me explain.

In today's globalized culture, we have coveted our individuality even when we don't call it such. We perceive ourselves to be innovatively progressing in our freedoms, and a diabolical situation has hence arisen:

> ***We have become so free, that we are increasingly unwilling to tolerate the freedom of others if their lifestyles do not mesh with our own.***

Yes, I did that...I just threw a metaphorical bone out for you to gnaw on. I suspect some of you reading along may be offended at my supposition. After all, are we as a worldwide community not becoming more and more tolerant every day to alternative ways of life unlike our own? Isn't that what we've been taught we must embrace? Great question, keep gnawing and while doing so, please think through one more challenge—having to do with the very definition of tolerance:

Referring back to Mr. Webster, we are told that *Tolerate* is a verb of allowance, permitting something to be done without prohibition, hindrance, or contradiction. In the simplest form, to tolerate something is to "put up with it."[15]

Correct me if I'm wrong, but I see nothing in that description suggesting I have to like, endorse, celebrate or encourage the tolerated behavior or action. But in today's environment, we are told that tolerance requires *inclusion:* a relation between two classes that exists when all members of the first are also members of the second.[16]

Really? How can that be possible? By such design are we not pitting an unstoppable force against an immovable object? Let me use a crazy but feasible example to make the point:

> Let's say I am a vegan and the sight of meat sickens me. I work in an office that is not near any eating establishments, so my employer has graciously put a cafeteria in the building. We are not allowed to carry or eat food outside of the cafeteria because we are a tech-firm that necessitates close to sterile working conditions. My co-workers like meat and are prone to consume it in my presence. I'm pretty high up in the food-chain (sic) of command, as a matter of fact; I invented some of our technology, so my position is crucial to our success. Therefore I decide to "pull rank" and demand that vegan dietary elements be required of all staff in order to tolerate my sensitivity.

I see this as very rational. After all; vegan food is good food. It offers all the nutritional value that a meat diet offers. I can't fathom a reason why others would not celebrate such a change in their lifestyle, can you?

What's more, in this fictional example, I'm perfectly willing to allow anyone who does not want to adhere to these conditions to find employment elsewhere. I don't own the company, but I'm a strategically integral part of its workings, so the company should have no good reason to deny my request, should they?


**WAIT A MINUTE…**

—Am I suggesting that some lifestyles are more tolerable than others? What about the carnivores? Are their rights forfeited by my value to the company and my supposed nature-conscious nobility?

---

[15] https://www.merriam-webster.com/dictionary/dictionary
[16] https://www.merriam-webster.com/dictionary/dictionary

### THE TRUTH OF TOLERANCE AND INTOLERANCE

Remember the Romans and how they began to embrace the very behavior actions they sought to punish? If we have become that system, it means ironically that we are rebelling against the very nature of improving our cultural circumstance through unifying discourse. How can that be? Why would we do that?

There are three emotional conditions that come to my mind for explaining this:

**Guilt**—*I feel badly that somehow my beliefs and actions have caused others to be marginalized.*

**Conflict Avoidance**—*As long as others beliefs and actions don't interfere with my own, I don't want to cause dispute or social struggle.*

**Convenience**—*I have my own life to work out, I have no time or interest in becoming involved with the issues of those unlike me.*

—Perhaps you can offer other condition examples.

In an immediate circumstance, being confronted with opposing positions and lifestyles, all of these emotional states make perfect sense. But over the course of time, at individual, community and global levels, all of them become corrosive to the fabric of our co-existence.

With each of us ignoring our differences for one reason or another, we become habitual in our practices and intractable as we use our beliefs and actions to cope against perceived enemies who intractably cope otherwise. This leads to individuals and groups creating defenses and borders; further isolating themselves in an effort to protect their "turf" rather than seek common ground. Ultimately, when two or more competing factions seek a similar objective, property or stronghold, instead of looking at ways to share or fairly grant ownership rights of said equity, they engage in another well-known pastime:

***War. verb—the act of laying claim to property and positions of belief by superior force[17]***

---

[17] I probably define this action a little differently than most, even Mr. Webster and I need to seek deeper understanding on this one.

To avoid that undesired activity, at some point we have learned to seek out compromise, a way by which highly contrasting factions can work and co-habit the planet without inciting devastation upon on one another. Mine was a fairly banal example, but serious conflicts have been waged for exactly this reason. Tolerability cannot win when one group forces its values on another. Ask religious groups and unions, genders, political affiliates, etc. We all want our cake and we want to take the cake away from anyone whose positions vary significantly from our own.

This is where things get tricky, because we have turned the phrase "understand" into "tolerate" and that phrase has been warped into "approval". Last but not least, we are now being taught by social engineers that "approval" must result in agreement, yet we do not agree. As a matter of fact the common understanding has become that we literally agree to disagree, turning a blind eye to the behaviors and beliefs we each find unacceptable. In other words, we have marginalized one another into disagreement boxes, all the time pretending we live together in a harmonized state of being.

Most countries across the globe share this falsely elevated sense of civility. We all pat ourselves on the back claiming we have achieved a populous-majority equilibrium. If so, then why do minorities continue to rise up, crying out for justice against their oppression? Are they marginalized? When given a platform, they too seem to marginalize, verbally and sometimes physically attacking the very people they claim to want dialogue with—displaying the very behavior of which they claim victimhood.

How is it that we have not already eliminated one another from existence? What has kept us from obliterating everyone else? For to be honest, there exists not one person on this spinning ball who shares an exact match of principles to another. How have we managed to achieve what we have?

## CHAPTER FOUR—A SCHEME FOR ALL AGES

*I want to stand as close to the edge as I can without going over. Out on the edge you see all the kinds of things you can't see from the center.* —Kurt Vonnegut[18]

[18] https://www.brainyquote.com/authors/kurt_vonnegut

I'VE ALREADY REFERENCED some prominent time periods, ancient cultures and people who have either marginalized or been marginalized. We now know the "what" of it, and the "why" of it. But what about "How?" Particularly; how do we shake off our attitude of marginalization?

### THE MARGINALIZED IN REAL-TIME

> Way back in my early teens, I had my first experience with horseback riding. I don't know if the stable-hands were trying to help or if they were having fun at my expense, but regardless, the horse which I was provided was blind in the left eye. The disability made him prone to walk in right hand circles which necessitated constant tugging on the left-hand reigns in hopes of a straight path. Of course the horse's name was Lefty and my first riding experience helped me understand that situations crop up where irony and parody can co-exist. More so, I came to recognize that, no matter how I might encourage Lefty in other directions, "right" was his determined path. The only thing that might have changed his perspective would have been some extreme revelation beyond my meager coaching or a great tragedy effectively obstructing his course.

I share this tale only to bring attention to our collective tendencies. We learn based on a combination of inherited and learned traits. We all have psychological or physical skills and impairments[19] which affect our mindset in ways we seldom recognize, except on the deepest of subconscious levels. To get me to break through my preconceived notions for a serious consideration of a new ideology, I would have to be shocked, positively or negatively into what I call *Humility Mode*. Because there seems to be a lot of confusion in the concept, I'm going to first make a clear distinction between the condition of humility within one's self, and the outward act of humiliating another. Even though observation of others suggest a common thread, I'm also going to limit my comments to my own history and let you make your own self-determination as to whether or not the shoe fits.

---

[19] Denying this fact is in itself an impairment.

Regrettably, when I either want to correct someone whose behavior or actions do not match up to my expectations, I usually cross a moralistic line by…

> *—reducing them to a lower position in my (and other's) eyes: attempting to create in my target, a sense of shame or embarrassment. I seek to mortify.*[20]

Mr. Webster defines these actions as *Humiliation.*

Sound a lot like a form of marginalization? I won't argue with you although I'll caution: don't think marginalizing is limited to this little piece of corruptible behavior. We'll get into its deeper forms later, but for now let's compare humiliation to a state of being, a freedom from pride or arrogance, a quality or state of being <u>humble</u>: What our favorite lexicographer defines as *Humility.*

What's my point? Since I'm keeping this personal, I'll admit that I'm all about shaping the lives of others with not enough consideration to the most important need, the adjustment of my own life. I might find the most convenient method to accomplish my objective is to embarrass or demean the person I'm trying to reform, into what I consider the best model for his or her life.

**WAIT A MINUTE…**

—Am I suggesting that the best intentions of man and womankind can be founded on the assumption that we, the marginalizers, are superior to we the marginalized? I'd like to claim only the role of martyr in all of this—maybe you would too, exclusively occupying the ranks of the pathetically marginalized. For myself, I know better—I'm just as prone to be the culprit.

What a confusing paradigm. It suggests that each of us can play the victim or victimizer at any given point to suit our individual and collective purposes. How can we get along at all when we're all not getting along? Perhaps a new order is in order.

**OUT WITH THE OLD**

---

[20] Merriam-Webster Dictionary https://www.merriam-webster.com/dictionary/humiliation

In fairly recent history as the clock of civilization goes, an intriguing societal concept gained favor. People began to resent that others were more privileged or more elite than they. Kingdoms crumbled and in their place democracies and republics of individual freedoms emerged. A new era arose where we recognized the value of one another's contributions mattered and a new word was used to define it—*Equality*.

Political, social, regional and yes, even religious organizations formed with the intent of better defining what it meant to be equal. New terms started emerging that rang sweet in our ears:

> Equal Opportunity
> Separate but Equal
> Equal but Diverse

Other terms surfaced, each pointing to a strange shift in our equality-groupthink, summarized in the following ideology:

*You can be equal in your way of thinking and living*
*as long as you let me be equal in my way of thinking and living.*

**WAIT A MINUTE…**

—Separate equalities? Can such a model exist? Is one equality better…more equal, than another?
Apparently at some point, we began to believe that these separate equalities/benefits could many times be equalized in value. We called this process *Negotiation* and began to enter into equality agreements where I would allow you what you considered to be fair in practice, as long as you allowed me the same. We started writing up these arrangements to keep track of them.

Let me detail the origins, evolution and current understanding of these promises:

> Fair trade agreements are referenced in historical documents dating back to Egypt and possibly earlier. Many early cultures helped perfect them. The Babylonians and the Assyrians traded their slaves using similar techniques. The ancient Jews called the practice *Meyshar—(an equal agreement) Separately Together*. The idea of mutual promises took deeper root via the Greeks. Through that society a cultural merchant class developed. Contracts evolved within that social structure as business/commerce promises with capitalistic objectives.
>
> But we can credit, or blame (your choice) the Romans for perfecting the contract concept. They coined a very basic phrase to define the essence of these governmental, geopolitical and business promises:

### *Quid pro Quo*

Sounds so fancy today, but all it means is:

### *Something for Something*

Today we call them…

### *Contracts*[21]

---

[21] https://www.britannica.com/topic/contract-law

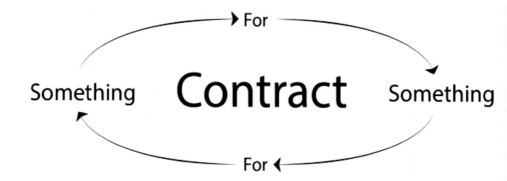

## WAIT A MINUTE…

—Am I saying that contracts, personal, governmental and or business in nature, are the means we deliberately use to marginalize one another? Exactly. These agreements of benefit are a subtly diabolical method, invented to, in appearance legally protect humans from being marginalized. Yet, by their very design contracts corrupts all hope of unifying their parties of interest. How is this proven out? Easily:

> Quid Pro Quo became the foundation for our contractual agreements and that sounds quite equal, doesn't it? Perfectly acceptable and right: right? After all, as the contract culture progressed everyone involved got what they wanted. Agreement language improved; legal terminology such as *caveats* and *stipulations*, *proxies* and *acceptances*, *bilateral adjustments* and *arbitration* came into play. Proof of qualifications became necessary for people who practice their trades under contract. Titles like *certified* and *licensed* became necessary to demonstrate the quality of one's abilities. Rules and ordinances dictated how we were to behave.

> And then something changed...

### —Contracts became the primary way we sought to enable relationships with one another

> Quid pro Quo was interwoven into everyday life. Contractual agreements leapt out of the business world and into families, schools, government and civil life. Everything became a contract. All parts of life became contractual. Wherein the past we married in the site of God and witnesses, it became necessary to have a civil license…permission by legal agreement. In days gone by, we could grow a crop, hunt for food, homestead a plot of land, and raise a family, but suddenly there were restrictions, deeds and negotiated terms necessary to conform to the wishes of the community. Quid Pro Quo became not just an accepted practice, but the law of the land.

> Somewhere along the way, someone thought, "I should get something extra, exclusive to what I want, out of an agreement." *Individuals trading purpose for purpose* then began to contract with one another, not toward a mutual understanding, but with a self-centered desire presumed to be of equal benefit to the other participant(s).

47

## MARGINALIZATION IN REAL-TIME

Fast forward to today to see just how much contract language shapes our lives. For the most part we bring our children into the world in licensed facilities with the help of certified individuals. We require graded school curriculum and expect graduation according to a prescribe method that proposedly benefit both students and the system the students will serve. Our jobs and the benefits of those jobs are outlined with employment agreements. Our government may invite voting of elected officials, but the bureaucracy that functions to provide for our infrastructure and social order is contractually based in laws and regulations that remain when the politician exits the stage. Religious organizations and faith groups agree to business and governmental restrictions, in some cases embracing regulations diametrically opposed to their doctrines. They justify their apologetic sacrifices in trade for not-for-profit tax status. Even our deaths are protected by life-insurance contracts and *Do Not Resuscitate* clauses which dictate the outcomes of our existence.

There is little, if anything that does not require contractual consent to function properly in the postmodern era and negotiation has become the art of who benefits most in any given circumstance.

So now, something else has changed...

### —*Contracts have become the primary way we seek to marginalize relationships between one another*

Our societal Quid pro Quo mindset has set us against one another, competing for who gets the better or best deal when entering into any arrangement. Shared benefit has become Yertle's tower with each individual trying to rise to the top of the heap of recognition and/or power. Party protectionism rather than mutual interest has become the concern of the day.

Ironic, is it not, that our efforts to include everyone in better practices, has actually led to greater marginalization by way of contractual barriers? Contracts are now our agents of marginalization and the primary inhibitor of truly equal rights.


### THE FALLACY IN CONTRACT THINKING

But why do I sound so anti-contractual? Marginalization risks aside, hasn't this approach served us very well over the years? Isn't our system thrived and are not our citizens guarded by the contracts in which we wrap ourselves?

## WAIT A MINUTE...

—Do you see how easily I pushed aside the marginalization risks? To be glib about it, I might have said, "What are the lives of a few people whose rights and dignities are pushed off to the side? A negligible act of cultural genocide; in the big picture, that's a small price."

How cold I sound. How dispassionate to those few, who actually are not so few. In fact they are, as discussed before; all of us. There is no such thing as a clean contract and therefore marginalization is not diminished but becomes the quest of the contract. What happens when the trade is...unequal?

Even though we may say we want to honor our contractual partner's interest, are we really willing to see a contract through if we feel we are getting a lesser deal? That's why another refinement emerged in the contract world that allowed for escape from the agreement. It involves a now familiar writing technique called the *Loophole.*

The loophole is nothing more than a clause written or a phrase left vague in the language of the arrangement that allows one or all parties to abandon ship. So that:

*If one or the other party backs out or fails to provide the agreed to efforts, the contract fails.*

But that begs the question, why would somebody; or everybody want to abandon a perfectly good ship that was not sinking?

I've already admitted in my own case as a self-imposed adolescent outcast, my isolation felt uncomfortable. I'm a social being just like the rest of us and would argue that there is a conflict within each of us that constantly struggles between separation from, and integration into, the pack.

## LOOPHOLE THINKING VERSES CONTRACT THINKING

And there is another ugly little secret I don't like to admit to when dealing in contracts. It is the intent with which I enter into the contract. In most cases, if not all, I am thinking ahead, trying to figure out if there is some way I can improve on my "deal" and also if I can back out of the deal after gaining at least some partial advantage. Of course I don't use that kind of language in my brain. I tell myself I'm just doing what everyone else does. I imagine that, if I don't sweeten the pot for myself, the "other party" might gain some undeserved advantage. So, why not "push" the system a little? We all do it, so we all should position ourselves for our own advantage, shouldn't we? That can't be the same as marginalizing because there is no way we can be at fault for out-smarting our neighbors and out maneuvering our adversaries. Then again who is our neighbor and who is our adversary? I seem to remember a certain itinerant preacher from long ago speaking to that issue.

## CHAPTER FIVE—The Consequences Of Marginalization

*If we aim a blow with a poker at a fly that perches on the forehead, we run a great risk of knocking out the brains.* —Anonymous[22]

---

[22] New Cyclopaedia of Prose Illustrations—Rev Elon Foster D.D. c1877

I WAS DEBATING ABOUT THE TITLE FOR THIS CHAPTER, thinking that *The Tragedies of Marginalization* best summarizes the content. By our actions we separate ourselves and that is tragic indeed. But thinking it through completely, tragedy suggests an innocence of responsibility and I'm promoting the premise that we are all very much culpable in the crime of marginalization. With responsibility comes consequences and that suggests we can change those consequences by owning our actions and our communal mindset. So let's talk about the consequences...responsibly.[23]

Since we've already concluded that marginalizing others is seldom a good thing,[24] let's consider the aftermath of our misdeeds. Here I'm going to touch on a very, VERY controversial example of poorly-played[25] marginalization.

**MARGINALIZATION IN REAL-TIME**

In 1955 a Jewish man observed his son participating in a school prayer and was repulsed because, in his own words, "That's not the way we pray." The man, Steven Engle happened to be a lawyer and cofounder of the New York Civil Liberties Union. He began a legal protest that would lead to a landmark decision by the US Supreme Court ruling that the school was infringing on the children's first amendment rights by setting aside compulsory time for group prayer in the morning prior to classes. The constitutional language used to support this point is:

*Congress shall make no law respecting an establishment of religion...*

---

[23] All of that consequentially responsible thinking makes me dizzy!
[24] Don't forget my warning about psychopaths
[25] My opinion.

Following this ruling against compulsory prayer in schools, two other rulings prohibited Bible readings in public schools. Fast forward to today and, regardless of your religious or moral leanings, there can be no arguing the numbers:

**Truancy and lower expectations in the classroom have noticably increased.[26] School shootings by students aimed at bringing harm to other students and teachers has dramatically risen.[27]**

**People's ability to articulate their faith has been curtailed through embarrassment, bullying and intimidation.[28]**

**Bullying as a method of intimidation/marginalization continues to be affect society.[29]**
**Crime statistics of those dropping out of the school system early has soared.[30]**

Are there other contributing factors? You bet and non-religious folk might argue that the removal of prayer and biblical readings were not valid factors in the rising stats. But there is no ignoring the signs of the times following the ruling:

*The culture we have created allows for unbridled actions on the part of the individual without first, the encouragement of critical thinking skills to govern such actions.*

I'll go a spiritual step further and suggest the following:

*Whether or not one believes in God is not the issue. It is whether or not one is encouraged to*
*honestly consider the existence of God without the pre-bias of those hostile to such a possibility.*

---

[26] https://www.brookings.edu/research/chronic-absenteeism-an-old-problem-in-search-of-new-answers/
[27] Read any newspaper, internet news-source or network news outlet; any day of any week.
[28] https://www.barna.com/research/barna-identifies-seven-paradoxes-regarding-americas-faith/
[29] http://online.ucv.es/wp-content/blogs.dir/15/files/2015/02/2012_DoneganRichard_Bullying-and-Cyberbullying_Articulo.pdf
[30] https://www.slj.com/2008/08/students/crime-linked-to-dropout-rates-report-says/

The bottom line is, certain people felt marginalized because they were told they had to worship in a particular manner to suit the majority. Let me be clear in my next statements and please read my entire reaction to understand my position: I agree with a ruling that prohibits the any civil requirement for common prayer or common worship. To my knowledge, God opposed it too. Read Luke chapter 20:23-24 for some clarity from that perspective.

Now let's tackle the more devious plot. We live in a secular society with freedoms and practices that should be allowed for all. So what's the problem? Our beloved Supreme Court of the land solved the situation, right?

I disagree. By protecting the rights of one objecting group we have gone and marginalized another group who believe they also have worshiping, educational and prayerful freedoms according to the second part of the constitutional article in question:

*—or prohibiting the free exercise thereof...*

**WAIT A MINUTE…**

—Do I dare suggest that the highest court in the land mistakenly substituted one set of freedoms for another? It wouldn't be the first time such a compromise has been made and the statistical facts support the results. For example: The freedom of speech versus the pursuit of liberty for all and protection of societal norms has always been a dance of delicacies.[31]

Whose fault is this? Oh, this is most probably where you will most definitely be offended: I submit that each one of us, particularly Christians, are at fault—not for allowing other's their freedoms, but for not demanding our own. I cannot find any landmark case where worshipers of Jesus do not insist on a private time of contemplation, celebration, prayer and study within the public system. Muslims insist, Buddhists and Jews insist. Where is the defense of my faith?

---

31

https://ir.lawnet.fordham.edu/cgi/viewcontent.cgi?referer=https://www.google.com/&httpsredir=1&article=2727&context=flr

**THE RESULTS**

By now I hope you've also come to realize a very basic, but profound fact—even with our best efforts:

*Each and every one of us is marginalized.*
*Each and every one of us is marginalized by each and every one of us.*

**ME AND YOU VERSUS THEY—SMALL THINKING VERSUS BIG THINKING**

So what if some of us just refuse to be inclusive? What happens when "They" really want to be an exclusive club and refuse to see the value in me—in you?

**THE MARGINALIZED IN REAL-TIME**

Here's one example of what can happen when those who should be "invited in" are intentionally kept out:

> In 1938 a young black man was sent to a juvenile detention home. There, supervised by a white couple, he admitted to good care, but also to being treated as if his heritage was a stumbling block, not a pathway. A turning point in his life came soon thereafter when this very intelligent boy shared his aspiration of becoming a lawyer, with one of his teachers. The teacher discouraged his quest, explaining all too kindly that he needed to explore realistic goals.
>
> School then became a restraint to him and he went to the streets, becoming a drug dealer and crime boss. Inevitably he was arrested and imprisoned, spending his time now in his own pursuit of education utilizing the prison's library to expand his horizons.
>
> Released after ten years, the man became the militant recruiter and subsequent leader for an activist organization that promoted separation of Black America from White America by any means possible. His civil rights cause encouraged open revolution by methods including violent uprising, to accomplish its goals.

Here's another example of someone under the same circumstances being encouraged to run with his dreams:

> This man was born into slavery, and, having been separated from his mother and father, was later adopted by his owners. They encouraged him in the sciences and he excelled, ultimately applying for college. He was turned away because of his race, but because of the support of his guardians and others, he sought alternative college opportunities, ultimately graduating with his Masters in Science.
>
> His higher degree would have itself been an astounding achievement to rest upon, but from that start, he became an accomplished botanist researcher, developing new cash crop opportunities for areas over planted in cotton. His work enabled black farmers' livelihoods and economic freedom they had never had before.
>
> Like the activist in the previous account, the botanist also spoke on civil rights, though his was a message of unity and equality for all.

The biographies of Malcolm X and George Washington Carver offer a stark contrast in how two similar men from marginalized backgrounds can be inspired to break free from oppression. Sadly, one chose to marginalize others as a means to his ends, while the later example found and promoted avenues of understanding to benefit all. The lesson includes a warning:

### *Be careful whom you marginalize, they may not like it.*

The tragedies and triumphs of the marginalized often reshape everyone around them. What a paradox considering the intent of marginalizing is to suppress, not enable. This brings up a valid point regarding our efforts to midrash. Do I have to like you to learn from you? Do we have to be in agreement to start seeking unity? As important can we by our efforts to unify in thought, affect the opinions of other groups who consider our efforts adversarial?

To be honest, I midrash with a lot of people who I ordinarily would rather avoid. In doing so, I'm tested, as are they. The result is either my satisfaction that my beliefs are strong, or my conviction to improve my understanding. Does that mean that my example will influence the behavior of others? Of course not! There is an underlying pattern associated with this reasoning that often goes unrecognized. Humankind revolts when things get too dictatorial. Others may not like what I think and they may react in ways I don't appreciate. If I insist that they behave as I do, I might find myself violently corrected. Ultimately the lopsided segmentation of the French Estate system led to the French Revolution, but not before infusing the concept of entitlement into the social mindset throughout Europe and beyond. Marginalization includes community, national, and even global causalities.

So how do we invite dialogue and possible change without inciting riot? As George Washington Carver might have offered:

> ***The promise of a healthy tree is in the proper planting and nurturing, not in the chopping down of someone else's tree.***[32]

No one wants to hear the fact that influencing others and being influenced by others takes time. It's too much trouble to consider alternatives. Whose side do you take? Who are "they" and who are "we"? Just pick a side and fight; right? And if I'm that intractable, how can I approach others unwilling to discuss another point of view?

What about tolerance? Shouldn't we all just let everyone have their own ideas without risk of confrontation? Ah, there's a tricky question. I have little or no tolerance for those who have little or no tolerance for me. So do I stand toe to toe with them, or…marginalize them. The latter is easier, but is it effective in the long term? Again think Mr. X and Dr. C.

It's challenging to think that we should be personally seeking and designing our lives around personal privacy, but are we capable of such effort? What if we simply don't want to pursue the course, or worse, what if we desire just the opposite—to purposefully diminish, possibly even destroy other souls?

**EXCEPTIONS**

I'm not sure there's any good place in this book to bring this up. I hate even having to think about having to bring it up. It is an obvious exception to our conversation about tolerance and marginalization of others. It has to do with psychopathic personalities[33]. Right to the point I want to say, these are not folks who can or that we want to try to work back into fellowship. There are just some physiochemical issues that are not yet curable and the psychopathic condition is that dangerous incurability. I don't want to spend much time on the problem except in warning. Until the time when there are legitimate remedies specific to psychopathology, those suffering the condition should most definitely be marginalized from the broader population: In my opinion; completely so. It's an ugly truth

---

[32] Actually this is a quote from me, not from him. But I'd like to think we were unified in the thought.

[33] Not to be confused with sociopathic personalities. See http://www.medicaldaily.com/whats-difference-between-sociopath-and-psychopath-not-much-one-might-kill-you-270694 for the distinction.

that there are those who have no restraint in their willingness to physically harm others. Someday perhaps there will be legitimate rehabilitative methods to alleviate the problem, but for now, sadly, isolation is all we have.

## WAIT A MINUTE…

—"What do you mean, Mark", you ask? "Are you suggesting these people are unredeemable?"

I suggest only that no modern-day documented redemption of any psychopath has been offered. On the other hand, that itinerant preacher I spoke about before, did succeed in creating true relationship with such a fellow. I suggest only that the itinerant preacher's methods of de-marginalizing were far more radical, and for us to attempt the same in this day and age will require a huge paradigm shift. We'll address that radical approach later on, but for now, just be open to the idea that playing with gasoline and fire without the proper training and approach will most definitely end in disastrous consequences.

## CHAPTER SIX—GETTING TO KNOW US

*"Granma said when you come on something good, first thing to do is share it with whoever you can find; that way, the good spreads out where no telling it will go. Which is right."* — Forrest Carter, The Education of Little Tree

*"And as you wish that others would do to you, do so to them."* —Jesus of Nazareth

JUST TO MAKE SURE THERE WAS NO CONFUSION IN THE MESSAGE OF CHAPTER FIVE; let me be real clear… our natural tendency is to not trust one another, so we designed a way to contractually keep one another at arms-length while concurrently holding one another accountable. But if you've really been paying attention and considering my arguments debasing contracts, I suspect a couple of new questions have been forming in your mind. Let me take a stab at guessing what they may be.

First of all:

**_If you have issues with the way things work in the world, what would you do to improve things?_**

Am I close? Let me try the second question that may have tickled your fancy:

**_If contracts didn't evolve until capitalism began to emerge, how did people come to agreements before that?_**

Both questions actually relate to one another, in my opinion, because I believe there was, and still is an alternative solution to our contractual way of existence.

**MARGINALIZATION IN REAL-TIME**

Back in the day…actually, way back in the day,[34] clans, tribes, towns and civilizations operated a little differently. Many of today's experts teach the rest of us based on folklore filters that imply those so-called primitive cultures of yore to have been more aggressive against one another, more tyrannical within their own borders and less valuing of the individual.

---

[34] So far back in the day in fact that let's call it, "the first day."

I'm not here to argue. There were undoubtedly, terrible examples of societal abuse in ancient times. Our legends, graveyards, written and oral testimonies speak to it strongly. What I would dispute is that we have improved, having somehow evolved into better replications of our ancestors. Here are some very modern-day numbers that should alert us to the unimproved state of our very human condition:

**Present-day Global Slavery: UNESCO Estimates that 45-50 million people are enslaved or involuntarily engaged in human trafficking.[35]**

**Present-day Global Conflicts: The World Bank estimates that 1.2 billion people, roughly one fifth of the world's population, are affected by some form of violence or insecurity.[36]**

**Present-day Global Totalitarianism: Approximately 3 billion people (40 % of the world's population) remain subject to elevated Authoritarian rule.[37]**

But in order to truly grasp the context of these statistics. Let's compare times present to times past, as best we can:

**Global Slavery: Anthropological research suggests the number of slaves per world capita has remained constant with the expansion of the world's human population. In fact, it may be actually increasing disproportionately.[38]**

**Global Conflicts: Looking back to the 500 BCE time period up to the beginning of the common era (year 0), the death and affliction rate was horrific with an estimated 20 million people being slaughtered in warfare. With the advent of more modern weapons, particularly looking from 1000 CE onward, the estimates for worldwide casualties has risen into the billions. Even excusing the fact that the total population has increased, the amount of carnage is far beyond a statistical growth norm.[39]**

**Global Totalitarianism: Although feudal kingdoms, patriarchal tribes and dictatorships have diminished over time, their reach and power over their controlled area has become more binding. Advanced surveillance, monetary controls, communication and travel limitations, along with educational approaches discourage revolution except when extreme hardships prevail.**

---

[35] https://www.globalslaveryindex.org/findings/
[36] https://www.theguardian.com/world/2015/may/20/armed-conflict-deaths-increase-syria-iraq-afghanistan-yemen
[37] https://www.economist.com/media/pdf/DEMOCRACY_INDEX_2007_v3.pdf
[38] http://www.historyworld.net/timesearch/default.asp?conid=1061&keywords=Slavery
[39] https://en.wikipedia.org/wiki/List_of_wars_by_death_toll

Of course the ancient numbers are not as easily corroborated as the modern-day figures. Some would argue that many ancient forms of slavery were touted as not slavery at all, but rather business arrangements of indenture, mutually beneficial to both owner and owned. Writers from the populations of the past who represented the masses under such agreements disagreed. I would tell the modern-day apologists of slave contracts that today's border immigration dispute in the United States and the Syrian Refugee migration to Europe (and beyond) are nothing less than acceptable forms of poorly veiled slave trafficking. We take advantage of struggling victims who willingly barter their dignity for survival in countries that benefit disproportionately from the available cheap labor pool.

## WAIT A MINUTE...

—Did I just suggest that our contractual way of life has turned into a system designed to disenfranchise/enslave certain contractual partners rather than protect them? If so, then that circumstance must have evolved intentionally, not accidentally. After all, contracts are most often carefully thought out, not accidentally achieved. What human being on this planet would stoop to such behavior?

Is there some internal desire wired into us to gain advantage over one another? Might that behavioral tendency be driving us toward, not away from marginalization? What if we actually thrive on the power we believe we have to categorize, organize and compartmentalize others? What if we believe social engineering to be our calling—what if we actually want to marginalize others?

This is a difficult pill to swallow. To think we are better is a part of our deep-seated individual pride. So the alternative—confession of our failures and then, the determination to change our condition—will take a greater work. In order to do differently, we must think differently. …. To de-marginalize we must seek a unified non-contractual mindset.

## THE DE-MARGINALIZED IN REAL-TIME

As mentioned in Chapter One, marginalizing behavior, though riding low under the radar in the Biblical narrative, reared its ugly head countless times in the early narrative—many famous and infamous characters chose to separate themselves from an overture or close communion; marginalizing others, and themselves. In Genesis twelve though, I read of a whole new relational paradigm taking shape that would, and still does, require a difficult choice—how and to whom do I choose to draw close to?

*Then the LORD appeared to Abram and said, "To your offspring I will give this*
*land." So he built there an altar to the LORD, who had appeared to him. From*
*there he moved to the hill country on the east of Bethel and pitched his tent, with*
*Bethel on the west and Ai on the east. And there he built an altar to*
*the LORD and called upon the name of the LORD.*
—Genesis 12:7-8

Why did Abe build an altar? What was this relationship with God all about? Did this behavior continue and did it affect the man's relationship with others—his clan and other relationships—as well? It's in this record that we can actually see the beginnings of a divergence from the norm, a new paradigm shaping. Abram will further commit to someone else's desire in ways not observed before—in any record, anywhere.

The changing seems to start in Genesis 14, after a successful battle against warring tribal leaders of the area who capture Lot, Abe's often beset nephew. Abram recovers his kinsman from ill fate and this is a first look at a new concept in its time. The concept is not a contract because Lot doesn't do any negotiating for his release. Abram recognizes that there is a benefit to everyone in his clan by the rescue. Everyone receives the same thing—unification and protection from nefarious forces, and the collective[40] is better situated for future expansion.

What should we call this new kind of arrangement, where the outcome benefits everyone equally? There have been societies and states, religions and organizations that pride themselves on the concept: It has become known as the *commonwealth* or \*common good*.

Dangerous territory that: To see a common good; someone has to determine whether or not… the good is actually Common. Just because one person sees it that way, doesn't make it so. Concluding the common good suggests dialogue: more dangerous perhaps is that to have dialogue, we need to do more than talk to one another, we must also listen to each other. More so, we must strive to understand what we hear and perhaps the most provocative of all:

**For the Common Good to become firmly rooted,**
**The majority must _agree_ on its commonality**

---

[40] OK, especially Lot, I'm sure he thought he got a better deal, but the better result was that other competing tribes learned not to mess with Clan-Abram after this battle.

In other words, we must all be seeking the same outcome for there to be a same purpose. I read Leviticus 19 again and concluded it to be someone's way of seeking a unified existence rather than a compromised co-existence of contractual marginalization. By the Leviticus model, thought now to be antiquated and obsolete, we first had to work at understanding our neighbors, then search for agreement together. There was no realistic way for two to approve of diverging lifestyles because each was predicated on foundational beliefs. Compromise was not an option; middle ground was not to be sought. All parties were to assume there was something more to be achieved; what was then called *higher ground.*

MARGINALIZATION IN REAL-TIME

A good example of a modern-day common good arrangement would be the Constitution of the United States of America.

> Before and during the conception of this document, there was great struggle and disagreement as to why the Western Colonies of England would seek independence. There was still hope held out that the King would come to his senses and invite a unified, equalized union. People in the colonies felt torn in their loyalties to the mother-country and concurrently a deep sense of marginalization. They were told they had honored status, but they were treated as if slave-labor subjects to the whims of others who did not take the colonist needs and abilities seriously.

> The resulting revolution and independence awakened in the newly formed United States, a common good that took hold and became the mind-set of the nation. Its tenants of agreement are clearly stated and immortalized for anyone wanting to understand how marginalization can both separate and inspire new unity:

> *We the People of the United States, in Order to form a more perfect Union, establish Justice, insure domestic Tranquility, provide for the common defense, promote the general Welfare, and secure the Blessings of Liberty to ourselves and our Posterity, do ordain and establish this Constitution for the United States of America.*

This *Preamble* to the Constitution of the United States defines the purpose of all the following structure. It presupposes a common good and that all participants are equally engaged; equally benefited with exactly the same rights and objectives. It does NOT (nor does any agreement for that matter) guarantee equal outcomes for all participants.

**Joining into a contract requires individual understanding between parties, and does not require common belief,**

**Joining into a common good requires common belief seeking common understanding.**

The language of the Preamble does not assign powers to a government nor does it provide specific limitations on government action and this is what distinguishes it from a marginalizing contract. Still the question: If it's not a contract, then what is it? Hold that thought. I'll come back to the terminology for this alternative later, but for now, check out the rest of the story. Taking a step back for a moment, remember our friend Abram?

SOMETHING GREATER THAN ABE

After the successful emancipation of Lot, Abram pays homage to a mysterious king—though there is no indication the king has asked for anything. By these actions; Lot's recovery and the freewill honoring of a higher power[41], a new thing happens that even Abram is not prepared for. In chapters fifteen and seventeen of Genesis, God claims Abram as his earthly recruit. He offers a unique relationship where God does the heavy lifting; gives the man a land grant and promises a vast lineage to come. God requires only worship and devotion and even puts Abram to sleep as a gesture indicating God alone will be responsible for the conditions of their relationship, knowing full well that Abe is not up to the task. God in essence de-marginalizes his choice representative, even renaming (by cultural standards—reclaiming by adoption) the man he had handpicked, now known as Abraham.

This ancient act is far different than that we examined with the common good scenario of the Constitution. Why? Although Abraham was a party to the commitment, he did not have the initial authority in coming up with the arrangement. A "greater power" or "higher authority" can sometimes inspire others to join in a common, but *greater good*. Yes, all participants have to ultimately unite in the cause, but it is beyond them, a concept that serves a purpose that typically involves a sacrifice of the common good for the greater good.

---

[41] *Suzerain*: a superior feudal lord to whom fealty is due

CAUTION: With a greater good understanding comes greater responsibility and greater trust. After all, there has to be a respect for whoever created the greater good arrangement as they had the initial vision (and should therefore best understand the long term intent). If there is a lack of confidence in the superior qualities of the higher power, then all bets on a unified effort are off the table.

Common good and greater good; constitutions and ancient commitments: What's the good and great of all of this? What's the big deal and why argue for or against contracts by invoking more primitive rites of agreement? Before I (finally) answer the question, let's make sure the distinctions are clearly outlined.

***Joining into a contract requires individual understanding between parties and does not require greater belief***

***Joining into a Greater Good requires Greater Belief seeking Greater Understanding***

And the new differentiation in the pursuit of a greater good...

***—Only one entity has to envision the existence and benefit of a Greater Good.***

Now that we've taken all the components apart and defined the differences, is there a name for this arrangement that offers both a common and a greater good? Are there other factors that differentiate it from a contract? You bet.

**MARGINALIZATION IN REAL-TIME**

Biblical and ancient historical records speak of another concept; one where both parties in a transaction seek a mutual understanding <u>and</u> agreement, <u>and</u> where all parties are seeking the same result/reward. The ancient term the Hebrews used to define such an arrangement was called *Bereth*[42]. It is a picture of two parties dividing up a sacrifice. In those days, an animal—agreed to by both parties as their common or greater "sacrifice"—was cut in half. The sacrifice would be laid out in the trench of a valley and the blood of the offering

---

[42]From H1262 (in the sense of *cutting* (like H1254)); a *compact* (because made by passing between *pieces* of flesh): - confederacy, [con-]feder[-ate], Covenant, league. Strong Hebrew dictionary

would be allowed to drain into the furrow. Both parties would then walk through the blood, agreeing that it was now their common understanding and that they shared all consequences. The severing of such an arrangement by either party would be as serious as severing a limb or taking the life of the other party—*your lifeblood is my responsibility, my life blood. We are **cut** from the same.*

Moreover, unlike a contract; if the agreement was breeched, the *covenant* remained to be fulfilled. Nothing would revoke it and it was up to both parties to restore faith in the agreement. If one of the participants remained faithful to the covenant and the other was unfaithful, it would have been the responsibility of the faithful to continue in faithfulness and offer to participate in redemption—restitution of a debt on the behalf of his or her failed blood partner.

The Romans also had a name for this kind of arrangement—*Foedus*. As a matter of fact there was even a Foedus arrangement documented shockingly between the Maccabees (later to evolve into the Jewish Pharisees) and Rome, inviting "friendship" with common purpose. Read 1Maccabees chapter eight (particularly verses 23-29) for the language which sounds remarkably like a covenant:

> "May all go well with the Romans and with the nation of the Jews at sea and on land forever, and may sword and enemy be far from them. If war comes first to Rome or to any of their allies in all their dominion, the nation of the Jews shall act as their allies wholeheartedly, as the occasion may indicate to them
> .
> To the enemy that makes war they shall not give or supply grain, arms, money, or ships, just as Rome has decided; and they shall keep their obligations without receiving any return. In the same way, if war comes first to the nation of the Jews, the Romans shall willingly act as their allies, as the occasion may indicate to them.
>
> And to their enemies there shall not be given grain, arms, money, or ships, just as Rome has decided; and they shall keep these obligations and do so without deceit. Thus on these terms the Romans make a treaty with the Jewish people."

Lots of other words originate from Foetus: Federation, Fealty, Loyalty being a few. And we certainly don't easily use terms like foedus or covenant today—they would sound too Archaic, Biblical/Spiritual chewed with our modern tongue. Instead we have given such declarations another name:

### *Treaty*

A treaty then and now would be visualized differently from a contract, looking something like this:

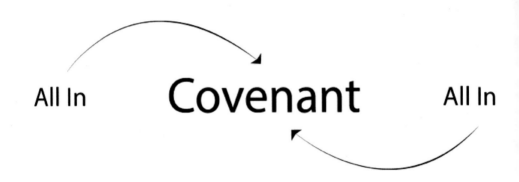

## COVENANT: THE OLDEST NEW IDEA

I'm thinking you have another question for me now. "If the idea of a covenant is so ancient and so good, why have we sanctioned contracts as our modern-day preferred form of agreements for society?"

Well if you haven't figured it out by now, Covenance takes a LOT of work! Is that what Abraham feared; his inability to live up to the task? Is that what we fear as well—why we sometimes are tempted to become invisible to our brothers and sisters because they…and our God might ask us to accomplish the *un-accomplishable*, sacrifice the *un-sacrificable*?

What might the un-accomplishable and un-sacrificable be? Well that depends on our own individual and congregational sacred cows, doesn't it? Am I; are we; willing to let go of the things we deem intractable in order to simply begin that honest midrash conversation? We spoke of the great risk of exposure in that "letting-go" early in the book, but there can be an even greater risk to pursuing such an approach. One party, or both may suffer injury in one form or another. Someone may even have their life taken in the effort.

We are only human. It doesn't take much for one of us to start mistrusting the other. And so we have become suspicious to the point where we expect, possibly even demand of one another a better arrangement, just in case one of us "messes up". Which raises one more question: Am I; are we even worthy of such a noble concept such as covenance; of being de-marginalized, being accepted into covenantial relationship; one with the other?

## OVERVIEW OF COVENANTS

To understand the value of covenantial relationships, we need to go back to the 30,000 foot view for a perspective. Imagine for a moment that there was no greater good, that we were all to conclude that, OK, Mark's right, let's all get along and come to a real solid common agreement. Let's take it a step further and imagine we came up with some amazing document such as the US Constitution and we all agreed it matched up with our core values.

Now imagine it's two or three hundred years down the road and someone among the ranks says, "You know what? We need to reexamine our agreement. There are a bunch of us who maybe don't agree anymore and we need to reword some of that old language."

Can you imagine the dialogue that would ensue; traditionalists insisting nothing change, new-age thinkers offering reformed ideology, anarchists throwing in controversial ideas just to "mix it up"? Of course you don't have to imagine this at all. It is happening before our very eyes and has been in fact happening since the days of the original constitutional convention. That's the blessing and the curse of a common good. It requires ongoing commotion to test its strength.

Continuing the value scenario, let's say that we all make peace with one another and continue with a common good arrangement. Then a new variable enters in…let's say, I don't know, maybe a meteor hits the Earth and all reverts back to those primitive tribal times.[43] Maybe there is no common interest and we are hyper-segregated in our thinking and our interests. Let's consider in this paradigm that there exists a benevolent dictator; someone who truly has envisioned the long-term consequences of a chaotic world order and has worked out a meticulous plan to make (not keep) peace on the planet.

Would the separated societies be able and willing to consider the future benefits of the monarch's plan? Would they share in his/her desire to surrender certain short-term comforts to see the plan through? What would happen if some, but not all of the world's population joined into the covenant? Or consider if there was an initial successful signup and then some of the participants later changed their minds and backed out?

Heady stuff: The difference in outcomes of such a covenant verses a contract would be profound. If a lack of, or change of participation does not change the nature of a covenant as it does with a contract, then the ideals of the covenant can never[44] be marginalized. And if marginalization is not a factor, then there is always an opportunity for non-participants to enter, or re-enter back into the covenant.

That's exactly what happened with the Israelites of old, who were somewhat famous for their zeal to enter into God's covenantial invitation, then realizing the sacrifices necessary, would abruptly bail out. The covenant(s)[45] remained available. The language in the literature consistently includes the phrase "everlasting". This type of interaction goes way beyond the scope of a common good as it requires a much deeper form of trust and reliance in the superior versus the inferior.

---

[43] Or maybe I'm trying to be so hypothetical that it will cause you to think way outside the box, and by doing so, maybe, just maybe you can hypothesize on your own that such a scenario might even exist today, without the interference of said meteor.
[44] —as in ever.
[45] Look them up sometime. There were a number of them that God offered to individuals and to groups.

**GREATER GOOD IN THE COMMON GOOD?**

One would think that a world filled with good contracts and good covenants would be a great place to live. And to think that suggests there must be some similarity or commonality between the two concepts that would lend themselves to one another. I did come up with one of those commonalities. It centers around a word already used heavily in this book:

*Relationship*

Going back to Chapter Four, I suggested that:

*—Contracts became the primary way we sought to enable relationships with one another*

That implies that there must be other ways that we sought…and seek to enable relationships with one another. And therein lays the commonality:

*—Both Covenants and Contracts seek to enable relationships with one another*

Wonderful: Now let's just examine the best covenants and the best contracts available and wrap them all together into a nice package. We can label our covenant/contract box, *"Can't We All Just Get Along?"*[46]

---

[46] Thank you, Rodney King.

## WAIT A MINUTE…

—"Mark, I seem to remember some issue you brought up about contracts that would cause that idea to crumble into a thousand pieces."

How illustrative of you to point that out. Indeed there was a follow-up construct to the point of contracts being our main relationship enabler.

*—Contracts have become the primary way we seek to marginalize relationships between one another*

So, contracts by their very nature cannot be enablers of relationship, but instead are the very disablers of sociable unity. Which brings up recognition of the key difference between covenants and contracts…

*—Contracts marginalize. Covenants de-marginalize*

The dichotomy between covenants and contracts only allows one of the relationship-means to exist at the expense of the other. Now then…

## WHICH SHOULD WE CHOOSE?

One would think (and I used to be one of those ones) that a covenantial agreement would in many ways be more marginalizing than a contract. After all, if I decide not to join in the fun, then I am excluded from the receiving the greater good prize in the end, am I not?

The difference is in who is choosing and whether or not the choice can be changed. In a covenant, I am the only one who can choose to marginalize and in truth, it is exclusively a self-imposed isolation rather than marginalization. If I don't want to participate, I have chosen exclusion, I have set my own terms for separation, and I am the only one to blame or to be damaged. The covenant continues and all involved, even if that is singularly the originator continue to benefit in unison. So…

*—Even if one party backs out or fails to provide the agreed to efforts, the covenant continues.*

72

In a contract, I have the same choice, but marginalization is most certainly evident. If I violate my end of that agreement, I have not only breached my benefit, but have nullified the contract itself. It cannot function without my participation, so I have marginalized all parties involved, breaking the contract and the objectives for everyone. No-one benefits and the contract ceases to exist.

To outline this simply…

## —Contracts marginalize, Covenants galvanize

### IS THE COMMON GOOD STILL GOOD?

"Seems to me, Mark, you skipped something. If the greater good is a covenant, what about the common good arrangement you harped on? Is it really good?"

—Great question. When parties can get together and serve a common interest, that would always seem to be a better arrangement. But here is one more dangerous question…anyone ever hear of the Communist Manifesto?

When Carl Marx and Frederick Engels published their positions, they also included a preamble. They spoke of a confusion that surrounded the concept of communism and took it upon themselves to articulate the actual definition. No problem there; to define something is always a healthy thing. The difference between the Communist Manifesto and the US Constitution however exemplifies what can go wrong in common agreements.

The Manifesto speaks directly to a Common Will, giving life to any groupthink circumstance. If a population therefore thinks something together, and acts it out, that's a good thing according to Marx and Engels. They were all about class struggle, so if one class rises up to supplant the interests of another class, so be it. All's fair in Common Will and the spoils go to the most imposing class.

Revisiting the Constitution; remember it speaks to Common Rights—Life, Liberty and the Pursuit of Happiness. This excludes no-one, but does require a cooperative atmosphere on the part of ALL classes.

Interesting, isn't it, that in theory:

> Both the US Constitution and the Communist Manifesto invoke a democratic approach where the agreement is brought about not by a superior authority, but a mass understanding? Both are common. Both propose to serve the public interest. But if we were to honor both of these ideologies within the same borders, there would not and could not be a common good. Their principles are in direct conflict with one another.

So back to the question: Is a common good really good? That depends on who is defining the good and the bad. It is why, to my understanding:

*A common good is only as good as the greater good that founds the common principles*

### WAIT A MINUTE...

—Did I just suggest that a common good has to be inspired by a greater good to be good at all? Yup, I believe that's what I just proposed. In order for a common good, shared by a population to be legitimate, it must be supported by a *singular* long-term plan, greater than the popular purpose of the common cause. So to put it Star Trekian terms...

*The Greater Good of the One best serves the Common Good of the All.*

But that means the common good of all is critically dependent on the greater ideal of the greater good. What if the greater good is ill founded and not truly good at all? Yes, what if indeed?

**THE MARGINALIZED IN REAL-TIME**

When my wife and I started researching ways to engage in unifying the economically and culturally marginalized of Williamson County, Tennessee we discovered that some unwritten rules shaped every aspect of our quest. We sought out churches and local charities. We institutional groups dedicated to officiating over the needs of the marginalized, we even reached out to individuals who had specific personal needs. The organizations and the marginalized themselves, in many cases indicated to us that:

*Giving money to a cause is wonderful*

*Offering time and resources to not-for-profit organizations serving the marginalized is noble*

*Praying for and discussing the needs of the marginalized is spiritually appropriate*

But:

*Offering to engage with the economically and culturally marginalized on frequent basis in true dialogue and daily living is very difficult and often discouraged.*

One group program that looked like a hopeful avenue for engaging with marginalized teenagers who were being abused by their families) invited us to join in helping. It would require us to go through a three week training course and commit to weekly availability— sitting in on court cases. Honestly we were very interested in the attempt, but the time commitment, our job schedules and the regulations of actual engagement were daunting. It seemed the system wanted to discourage actual engagement with the marginalized and encourage structure to keep the process *safe and orderly* for the common good of all involved.

Safe and orderly—The concept caused me to consider yet another paradigm shaping question:

*Is covenance—the pursuit of a greater good—a safe and orderly process?*

The question itself offers a comparison of covenants to contracts. Contracts by nature are meant to inspire surety, comfort that *if* all parties comply with the terms, *then* the outcome will be a completed agreement. Covenants offer no such claim. They by nature are ongoing and in a manner of speaking, always in search of completion. Because of this distinction, there is a riskiness suggested with covenants. They require more maintenance and longer-term commitment meaning that those who walk away for a covenant abandon the benefit, exposing themselves to less beneficial alternatives with required consequences outside of the protected collective. Those abandoning a contract may incur a penalty, but once settled they are not subject to any requirements. And then there is that difficult thing the Israelites learned about covenants. Covenants require personal sacrifice.

So, covenants are not safe havens and there is a requirement of, for lack of a better term, putting skin in the game. Does that make them a lesser choice?

## DON'T FORGET THE GREATER GOOD

There is another benefit in covenance not found under contract arrangements: Hope. By clinging to the covenant approach, in the end the committed group is commonly bettered. But the price can be high. And because of that hope, there are parties willing to struggle for the greater good.

## MODERN-DAY COVENANCE IN REAL-TIME

I can't think of one example of a modern-day covenant that is not based in at least a 2000 year old pact-of-old. You're welcomed to contradict me; careful though, remember the close resemblance of common good to greater good and the characteristics of each.

Come to think of it, there is one specific example I can offer of a personal nature. It contrasts well with the more contractual example mentioned above concerning abused children.

> Another organization that my wife and I ultimately did become actively involved in, addressed the needs of teens in troubled situations. The youth may have acted out in school or had been arrested or caught with drug paraphernalia; some had simply been neglected by parents. All, sadly, lived in one of the wealthiest, most productive places in the United States. You guessed it—Beautiful Williamson County, Tennessee.

The organization offered services to the teens and their families at no cost with only the invitation to *join in*. They provided sports activities, tutoring, social gatherings, and (where we became involved), self-expression/self-discovery sessions designed to encourage the kids to explore more about their inner desires and conflicts.

The program required no contractual agreement and only asked the participants to help one another learn how to communicate their desires and their frustrations in ways that others could easily understand. If along the way they chose not to participate, that was their prerogative, but they were asked not to interfere with the others' exploration. Everyone had the same goal: A greater good that the whole group could understand; expressed in the question:

### *How can I discover and best tell you who I am?*

Seems like a simple quest, but notice there was no *approval quotient*[47] evident. The objective was not to seek acceptance (that comes later with interaction), but only to be able to articulate one's thoughts and actions in ways that others could actually comprehend.

I won't get into the incredible results derived from this effort—that might be another book in itself—but do want to point out the covenantial aspects. The plan was not to get one person to understand another, each then getting some sort of individual reward, but to have all the participants learn the same skill and receive the benefit together.

### *All for the same purpose—all for covenance.*

Now you have a bonafide example of a modern day covenant in action. And we've gone through a pretty extensive litany of contract and common good characteristics. Maybe then, a rundown of covenant and greater good characteristics is in order.

---

[47] Rather than give Approval Quotient some pithy definition, I'll simply explain it in other terms later in this chapter. Look for *External Expectations* and *Internal Expectations*—you'll get the picture.

**COVENANTS AND CONTRACTS: CHARACTERISTICS AND COMPARISONS**

To do this right, we may need to include some further comparisons. First, remember that a contract involves a trade – something for something. There are actually covenantal elements in a contract, therefore, in that both parties are agreeing to work <u>toward</u> something verses an already achieved and agreed to pact. A covenant is more expansive than is a trade.

Contracts exclude non-participants and seperates partipants by agreement. Therefore a contract marginalizes all involved whereas covenants invite unity of all parties, even those outside the covenant, constantly offering participation. So a covenant is the opposite of marginalization.

Contracts are competitive by design—covenants are non-competitive by design. Really? How is this proven out? Read through any well written contract and you will find all participants throwing around the terms *Whereas* and *Therefore*. Most scholars and law-folk will tell you that this is clarifying language, and who am I to disagree? But whereas it may qualify the terms, it also suggests a competition—one against the other. Covenants typically involve another grouping of words: *Because* and *Therefore*.

What's so important about Whereas verses Because? Glad you asked. First, if you haven't figured it out yet, language is critical to any agreement, binding or loosening the arrangement in very specific ways. Therefore, when the word Whereas is used, a contrast is being established—*This* as opposed to *That*—again setting up a competitive arrangement. When the word Because is used, a *Cause and Effect* is established—suggesting that an outcome is dependent on a previously applied action.[48]

Both contracts and covenants use the term *Shall* implying a requirement from all who join in. This is a commonality between the two. After all, *Whereas* when one is seeking to marginalize another, they want to set up expectations that *Shall* allow for the separation (contract language). On the other hand, *Because* the expectation is to de-marginalize by a covenant, there *Shall* be an effort to include a same-for-same benefit.

---

[48] https://english.stackexchange.com/questions/124906/can-you-use-whereas-as-a-substitute-for-because

Covenants may be conditional or un-conditional. Contracts are always conditionally based. This means that sometimes with a covenant, there may not be any additional requirements other than to enjoy the mutual benefits of the greater good. Want an ancient example? Go to Exodus 6:6-8 in that book I keep referencing:

> *"Say therefore to the people of Israel, 'I am the LORD, and I will bring you out from under the burdens of the Egyptians, and I will deliver you from slavery to them, and I will redeem you with an outstretched arm and with great acts of judgment. I will take you to be my people, and I will be your God, and you shall know that I am the LORD your God, who has brought you out from under the burdens of the Egyptians. I will bring you into the land that I swore to give to Abraham, to Isaac, and to Jacob. I will give it to you for a possession. I am the LORD."*

Notice there is no expectation of reciprocation in God's declaration to Moses. It is assumed here that God is taking care of all the conditions. Granted, he may make requests later on the journey, but disobedience to those later *commandments* does not forfeit the original pledge. Show me that kind of arrangement in a modern day contract. No, as a matter of fact I can tell you right now that any contract requires repercussions when breeched. That is one of the contract's attractive features.

### *If I mess up the relationship, you get to punish me.*

Another way of saying this is that covenants are positively incentivized whereas contracts are negatively incentivized.

And don't forget common good arrangements in this comparison. Remember they are simply extensions of covenants, not existing for long without a greater good supporting them. Remember, I said I can't think of a modern-day covenant not based on a model already created long ago. Not even the Romans thought, and certainly not we today think or behave in such a way. Why should I do something that does not offer me the opportunity to receive a reward specific to my individual wants or need?

Saying all of this, I'm going to get a lot of un-fan mail from some of you regarding a modern institution that you will argue is indeed a covenant. We call it *marriage.*

**WAIT A MINUTE…**

—"Why isn't marriage a covenant, Mark?" You ask. Well, the <u>ancient</u> rite of marriage certainly was a covenant. But who would argue that the current world-view of marriage has changed? After all, the ancient rite was primitive and based on archaic principles, correct? Forgive my attempt at sarcasm, but I doubt if I would get much push-back from most reading this book; that, as defined, a true covenant is based on a greater good conceived from a *higher*, bestowed to a *lower*. So which is it, covenant or *conve-not*?

First, I want to state clearly that I dearly want marriage to be covenantial. The dilemma is that our society has done to matrimony what we have done to all other agreements. Yes, you guessed it—we have turned marriage into a contract. We have even designed contractual ceremonies, officiates, forms and licenses to civilly legalize the bond.

Ironic, no? We claim that marriage is meant to join two people together, yet we have contractualized…marginalized the sacrament and those associated with it; requiring governmental imposition and permission. We even offer prenuptial agreements to protect one marriage partner from the other. Does that sound like a covenant concept where everyone is participating equally? If a marriage arrangement is approached as had once been the case, none of these marginalizing restrictions would be necessary.

In this day and age, marriage is so mangled by politically correct ideology and contemporary interpretations regarding who marriage is between; that it would be safe to say there are no Superior and inferior considered to be necessary. Therefore I have to conclude that by humankind's modern standard, marriage does not currently reflect a covenant relationship.

What can we do to reinstate the proper approach to wedded bliss or for that matter any contemporary attempt at forming a covenant alliance? I will address that in the last chapter but will now say this; it all begins with equality.

**EQUAL BENEFITS VERSES EQUAL OUTCOMES**

Have you happened to check out Mr. Webster's definition of equality lately?

**: regarding or affecting all objects in the same way : <u>IMPARTIAL</u>**[49]

---

[49] https://www.merriam-webster.com/dictionary/equal

Where contracts and covenants come into play, the question of equality becomes one of competitive versus non-competitive outcomes. Do contracts and covenants differ in the kinds of outcomes they provide? Absolutely. Are those outcomes always equal?

If an outcome is contractually based, it will be competitive in conclusion. For example, as a writer I have all the same access to libraries of history and databanks of information. I have experiences as rich and varied as many others. But I am not Shakespeare or Shelly…nor are they me (for what that's worth). We have the same material to work with, the same basic intellect and writing skills, but each takes those benefits and either masters or abuse them according to choices and influencing events.

If an outcome is Covenatially based, it will be non-competitive in conclusion. As an example, if I am committed to serve the poor in Williamson County, Tennessee and others agree to join in with my approach, we cannot be in competition for the result. The result will be Because of our mutual concern for a greater good, not Whereas the poor will get one benefit and we the providers will obtain another.


**WAIT A MINUTE…**

—"Mark, it sounds like you are trying to associate the term contract with competing forces."

I am.

"Furthermore, you seem to be implying the covenants are non-competitive in nature."

That is true.

"Therefore, are you tying marginalization to competition and de-marginalization to non-competition?"

Nope.

"So are you suggesting that competition is not the best method for singling out exceptionalism?"

What I am saying is that there are two forms of struggle that we need to examine together. Over the course of civilization, one of these forms has caused a dramatic shift in the way we interact with one another; the other form has to do with the way we were originally wired to relate. One way leads to *contractual confrontation* while the other has everything to do with *covenantial coexistence.*

## EXTERNAL VERSUS INTERNAL EXPECTATIONS

I'd like to ask you a question. Is there a difference in the way I should treat others for their behavior contrasted with the way I treat the consequences of my own behavior? The politically correct response should be, "of course." But then again, what do we actually observe happening in the world? Before addressing the question in detail, it should be noted that the following discussion is not meant about competition verses cooperation, though initially that may be how it appears. In coming up with a good parable, research kept taking me to explanations that contrasted the two, when in fact I believe them to be separate societal behaviors all together. To me, the reality is that competition is necessary, but misdirected when posed outside of oneself. While cooperation always addresses two forces that make a symbiotic choice to mutually benefit. Hopefully, you will see in the next segment how these constructs differ and impact marginalization.

## MARGINALIZATION IN REAL-TIME

> **"Why do you see the speck that is in your brother's eye, but do not notice the log that is in your own eye? Or how can you say to your brother, 'Let me take the speck out of your eye,' when there is the log in your own eye? You hypocrite, first take the log out of your own eye, and then you will see clearly to take the speck out of your brother's eye."**

> —Gospel of Matthew 7:3-5

I've been as prone in my life to cut in front of the line to get what I want—a better seat at the movie theater; a more prestigious job position—there are lots of illustrations to point to and so I won't bore you. And to be gracious in allowing you to compete, please let me know which of us has not. That may seem like a harsh comparison and invitation, but it's meant only to drive home the point. We all want to be better. That's a good thing, of course. But now I'll ask you...

*"—better than what; better than whom?"*

If our quest is to outshine all others, where will that eventually lead? The only logical conclusion is that in competing, one against the other, one of us has to ultimately strive to be "the" Superior. Any other conclusion to External Competition would be a ruse.

Before you ask (again) if I think therefore competition is a bad thing, I'm going to open the paradigm-changing box again and pull out a new term:

### *Internal Testing*

I have had a love for running in my neighborhood for many years. Observing me in those frequent hikes, my well-meaning friends and neighbors have commented, "Why don't you run in a marathon. I never really had a desire to do so, but had difficulty articulating, "Why?"...

—So one year I gave in and signed up for a local 5K run. It was a mistake from the beginning. I shared with my encouragers that I'm not built for speed, just locomotive comedy. They assured me that all I really needed to do was run the race and not worry about how I looked or in what place I finished. That was only partially true.

When the race began, I had in my mind to do what I always have done, run, with the intent of improving my personal health and enjoying the natural progress of movement on a beautiful day. But the crowds on either side had other ideas for me. They kept shouting, "Come on, you can do it!" *Do what*? I was already doing it. "Pour the steam on," one person pepped. "Pass her, pass her," came a cry from an admirer who suggested the woman running ahead of me was actually an obstacle.

I was not the last in the ranks, but I certainly was not near the first finishers either and found my enjoyment of the run distracted by the masses' desire to have me surpass their expectations of my performance. What they didn't know was how driven I was by a deeper internal motivation.

As a child, I had severely pronated ankles—meaning they turned inward, causing a recommendation from a doctor to avoid the exercise of running long distances in order to protect my ability to walk correctly later in life. If I had listened to his competitive suggestion; i.e., "Be the best you can be later by simply surviving now," I most likely never would have discovered the joy of running. Here's where the tale gets tricky. I decided when the doctor gave his prescription, that I would not be limited by the expectations of others. There was only one I had to strive to outdistance and that was me. Ultimately, I learned that others typically did not have my higher objectives in mind, but were envisioning themselves in my efforts.

That's fair, we all compare that way, but I then discovered that I can't motivate others, nor can they motivated me. Motivation is internally inspired, not externally coached. Parents, family, friends, teachers, co-workers all tried to teach me otherwise and the more I observed their desire—to somehow influence me toward their aspirations—the more I realized my thoughts and actions were in danger of being externally distracted. Was that a bad thing? Only when the interests and insights of my encouragers verses my own aspirations was in conflict…as it often was—as it often is now.

Are you the same? Do you find yourself trying to please others according to their desires, not your own greater pursuits? Let's get back to the race…

—As I strove up a respectable hill on my quest to complete my 5K excursion, I found my thoughts to be much different than when I usually ran. Instead of being thankful (as was my normal thought process) that I had overcome my disability, simply enjoying the idea that I could run daily, constantly testing and satisfying my own inner motivations; I caught myself hoping for a quick finish to this ordeal, staged to make others feel better about how they had helped me.
That was the last race I have ever attempted to compete in.

**WAIT A MINUTE…**

— "Oh Mark, they weren't trying to hurt you, what's the big deal? Why are you so offended?"
Offense is not taken. What I took from that race of discovery was that everyone in a competition either for the benefit of others, or against the benefit of others, was striving to be superior.

"What? How did you arrive at that conclusion?"

By the simple act of projecting one's own aspirations onto another, we marginalize the other person's own quest for accomplishment. The choice of how we include rather than exclude, is up to us and leads to some odd logic: If we are looking for ways to include others in society, at some point we must exclude our methods of segregation.

Some of you might now want to argue that sometimes, the other person, the target of our well-intentioned management, may not be driven to accomplish anything. I agree with that, and there are certainly times when that person would benefit from inspiration (the example of others doing for themselves) rather than motivation (the intentional attempt to infuse one's personal aspirations into the life of another).

"Are you suggesting, Mark that there is no one worthy to be called a Superior to another? There is no one we should want to covenant with?"

Hang in there, Chapter Seven is just around the corner. Meanwhile, in comparing external competition to internal testing, there are clear differences. One is all about how I compete with others and the other is how I strive to become what I am designed to be within. And there is one more very significant variance involved with external competition versus internal testing (this is where I'm going to become unpopular):

*External competition is the only way to identify group external expectations and identifying external expectations is just another way to marginalize*

Whereas

*Testing is the only way to identify internal expectations and identifying internal expectations is the only way to establish a covenant*

How can I claim such things? What about our love for sports and academic excellence and national pride and on and on? I am not saying any of these things are bad, but they do separate us, and by doing so, we can never truly be united. It is reality. It is what it is.

Please do not get me wrong—I am not suggesting that we dumb-down our society by robbing individuals of their skills and accomplishments. But admit it: Once we celebrate our "wins", we seem to lean toward pushing others' struggles away as "not quite good enough". Is that true? By our success do we relegate others to failure rather than encouraging a shared experience? How can such a mindset possibly serve a greater good?

### WHAT'S THE FIX?

Throughout all of this academic banter, one question has not (yet) arisen. What can we do about the paradoxical conflict between a *contract mentality* and a *covenant mentality*?

Certainly we're not going to want to change our arrangements in midstream. Especially in a stream that doesn't seem to have too many dangerous rapids to maneuver. Covenants were a nice idea for the ancients, but we simply can't turn the clock back, right?

## WAIT A MINUTE…

— "Mark that means humankind is committed to marginalization and actually desires to be separated, one from the other. Is that a healthy thing to leave unresolved?"

No, it's not healthy and when I'm sick, sometimes the healing agent is not pleasant or immediate. It may take effort and longsuffering to make the change. That's why most epiphanistic revisions throughout history happen only when public opinion, massive need or cataclysmic shifts of power occur. Sometimes the change requires help from a force outside the recognized realm of possibility.

In the case of refocusing society from a contractually marginalizing mindset to a covenantially de-marginalizing mindset, such a change agent is known to exist. A redemptive approach was actually woven into the superior characteristic of covenant living.

Therefore, contract living tolerates nothing less than a rigid code of conditional obedience. But because of the relational flexibility built into covenant living, new covenant enhancements can readily be integrated.

## COVENANT COURSE CORRECTIONS

For a moment let's go back to the idea that only one entity has to conclude whether or not a greater good exists. This can obviously present a problem because, if no one else envisions the Good as Greater, then it's up to the higher power to invite and attract others to become involved in the purpose represented by the greater good. Regardless of the true value of the greater good, there may or may not be an attraction to "join in" on the part of others. The resulting rejection by the "lessor" party may be seen as a form of *reverse marginalization* and that is simply inaccurate. Think about it. To marginalize someone or a group, there have to be contractual conditions separate benefits that everyone is allowed to choose or reject. In the case of a covenant, there is only one condition and one invitation that remain open-ended. There is no rejection of parties, only the potential of rebellion concerning the cause. I may not like what the superior party has proposed and there lays the conflict. I either have to embrace the cause, or join in reluctantly or chose a path completely outside of the covenant. There is no negotiation to be had as there is in working out a contract.

## WAIT A MINUTE...

—Am I suggesting there are such things as conflicting covenants?

Well I didn't say that exactly, but if I'm somehow able to find two competing superiors, then yes, there would be a choice between covenants to be made. What is improbable would be for one superior to have devised multiple covenants that conflict with each other.

How do I validate the above stated argument?[50] If a covenant Creator is truly Superior, by definition, they would not be able to formulate such a contradiction. Covenants are never-ending remember, so any new arrangement has no choice by to adhere to the previous commitments.

PS Strange, isn't it; that at some point there can only be <u>one</u> Superior?

And coming right back to the idea of competing agreements, what happens if a covenant arrangement I enter into conflicts with a contract agreement I enter into? Well at that point I guess I have a very difficult choice to make, don't I? It would suggest that I'd better be very selective and discerning as to the arrangements and agreements I enter into. Any conflict might be very hazardous to my wellbeing!

*In a Contractual Culture, honoring a covenant, especially a covenant that may conflict with contracts considered more valued to the Status Quo, can prove a rocky road indeed.*

This is why it is crucial to understand the purpose of any covenant. All involved need to agree with the desired outcome. If one participant does not recognize the benefit, they will be reluctant, even rebellious toward the stated outcome. And that is where humankind fumbles, marginalizing others as the Romans demonstrated, coming up with new rules and new desired outcomes based on someone else's selfish needs. Such adjustments don't necessarily look wrong when promoted, especially when the participating partners can all successfully negotiate some additional benefit for themselves.

---

[50] Get ready; more paradoxical thinking about to be invoked here.

Now, understanding the deeper discovery related to our discriminatory tendencies—how marginalization is the outcome of *one-verses-the-other*—there are a few more things to reinforce before heading to the best chapter in the book:[51]

Covenants never go away: Once a covenant is struck, the journey toward a unified benefit is begun and can't be reversed. Remember, just because one party turns of the path doesn't me the other cannot continue. So if a covenant continues, there is always opportunity to redeem the real problem; that being *the abandoning covenant participant.*

Contracts are simply misinterpreted covenants. Properly reviewed and reconstructed to serve the greater good, most contracts can become superior covenant relationships. But with this understanding, comes a caution. Just because someone is willing to agree to the terms of a well-defined (for them) contract, doesn't mean they will be equally willing to join into an equally well-intentioned covenant that replaces said contract. Some people want *Quid Pro Quo* and may actually be repulsed by the idea of *All for the same purpose.*

With all this being said, it is imperative for me to understand the depth and implications of any agreement—covenant or contract that I may enter into. It's equally important that I research the characteristics and qualifications of any Superior with whom I might want to covenant. And that raises the most compelling question of all:

### *Who is qualified to be Superior?*

---

[51] Did you just catch how I baited that hook?

## CHAPTER SEVEN—WHO'S IN CHARGE?

*True strength lies in submission which permits one to dedicate his life, through devotion, to something beyond himself.* —Henry Miller

I'M GOING TO START THIS CHAPTER OFF WITH A BOLD APOLOGY. I suggested earlier that this would be the most exciting part of the book and indeed, if you've been following along closely, you will shortly recognize a radical change in my approach. For one more moment however, I'm going to internally test your patience to the hilt in order that we can explore some profoundly new territory.

Recalling how covenants differ from contracts: There is an implied common purpose, not a trade, wherein the parties agreeing to the covenant bind themselves to fulfill certain conditions to the mutual benefit of the participating parties. Such a binding requires a deeply personal relationship between all involved.

If the lessor party is willing to trust the Superior's prowess, then all things covenantial move forward swimmingly. But by the very nature of a covenant, sacrifice is necessary and over time, the trust is tested. Human beings just don't like waiting on sacrificial outcomes.

*At the point when the greatest sacrifice is required, the greatest doubt is demonstrated by the lessor covenant partner toward the actions of the Superior covenant partner.*

And at my sacrificial tipping point, covenant cooperation is most likely to break down. What does that look like exactly? Simple: the lessor covenant partner will call into question the authority and ability of the Superior covenant partner. And that raises another question: Does the doubt of the lessor party diminish the authority/ability of the Superior?

Here's where we take a sharp turn from accepted social constructs. Remember I asked at the end of Chapter Six, how can we determine who qualifies as a reliable covenant superior? If I want the answer to that question, I should probably have a superior idea of what defines a superior, right?

Starting off, good old Mr. Webster has already weighed in:

**Superior**    **1: situated higher up: UPPER**

                **2: of higher rank, quality, or importance**

I'll weigh in on this one because of the unique qualities associated with superiority. Let's check them out together:

**Attributes of Superiority:**

| | | |
|---|---|---|
| **Dominance** | **Perfection** | **Preeminence** |
| **Command** | **Sovereignty** | **Rule** |
| **Prerogative** | **Prominence** | **Greatness** |
| **Infallibility** | **Omnipotence** | **Predictability** |

In other words (as if I haven't used enough superior terminology), a Superior is above all.[52] And there is one additional distinguisher: being superior, suggests a rank. One thing or entity can't be superior unless there is something/someone who is inferior. Even more striking; to rank superiority means there must be a *most* and a *least* superior. Who gets to choose the objects and parties that merit said distinctions?

In my little universe, I have unsuccessfully categorized many other individuals whom I have deemed more or less worthy than myself. I can safely say that in 99.999% (ad infinitum) of the cases, I was mistaken and found that out because of that nuisance known as *time*.

Time allows for each of us to display the good and the bad of our behavior. There has been no example but one, over time that has displayed a dependable example of superiority. And that irks the rest of us because of that competitive component, we inferiors insist on continually kneading into our cultural dough. Can you see the contradiction? Competition has its own attributes, not the least of which is the inability to honestly recognize and completely respect the superior nature…of the Superior.

No, I did not call you (or myself) *dishonest*—that's for each of us to determine in our heart of hearts (by internal testing). However, I have proof positive that we are *disabled* when it comes to everyone's[53] recognition of superiority. The evidence is molded into a well-known construct integral to our interactions with one another—imbedded into our contractual DNA. We cling to this cornerstone because of our fear of living without it. We strive to live above it only to find ourselves guilty by peering into the convicting reflection of its mirrored structure. We love and hate the regulation by which it defines the righteousness and rebellion of our actions. I'm referring of course to…

---

[52] Notice how I capitalized all the attributes? Must mean they're pretty important, huh?
[53] Even the best of the best of us

### —*Law*

With law we measure not just our competitive tendencies, but also meter out judgement…competitively according to our individual and group perceptions of the common good. And by that deliberation, we also compare ourselves (aptly or inaptly) to the image of our Superior.

Remember also back in Chapter Six, the comparison between External and Internal Expectations was made, and I delayed answering the following:

> ***Is there no one worthy to be called a Superior to another?***
>
> ***Is there no one we should want to covenant with?"***

So here's the answer:

### *A Superior exists*[54]

By the way, besides the fact that I often times capitalize the word Superior, have you noticed that it is mostly referred to in the singular? Yes, there's a reason and that reason will (finally) help me bring the main point of superiority home:

***In truth and by definition, there can only be one Superior. And that truth leaves the rest of us inferior.***

---

[54] I'm not sure I emphasized that epiphany adequately. Let's add some exclamation points in there for emphasis—***A Superior exists!!!***

**WAIT A MINUTE…**

—"Mighty smug of you, Mark."

Well that might have been true had the definition been mine in the first place. But like the universe, there was an origin of this superior idea and it emanated long before I took a first noisy breath.

How are we even able to conceive of the idea of superiority? Since none of us realistically are, or ever have been superior, there had to have been some early perception instilled from some example. Have we always been, for lack of a better term…less? Has there always been a higher power that is distinctive and unmatched by even our best efforts—a Superior apart from us?

Is that even a remote possibility?

**MARGINALIZATION IN REAL-TIME**

The ruling class of the time would not tolerate the idea of an entity higher than their own authority having an actual intimate interactive with the masses. The religious leaders maintained their importance through rites and laws. For their own interests, the anti-establishmentarians sought some way to overthrow those powers.

But there was one humble yet confident one who had another vision or relationship with the people: All people. His purpose was not to unite the crowds for insurrection, but to join any who were willing, in a new venture, counter-culture to all other societal ventures. He envisioned a spiritual kingdom connected by two very simple principles:

> *Love the Lord, your Superior, with __all__ your heart and all your mind*

> *Love your neighbor as yourself*

> —Transliteration of Deuteronomy 6:4 and Leviticus 19:18

—Such simple and elegant ideals. Even if someone doesn't believe in God; certainly they can appreciate the depth of devotion, the power and passion of the kind of faith it would take to love a Superior so completely. Even if someone is absolutely anti-social or prefers the hermit's model; certainly they would be overcome if someone else loved them so deeply.

That "one" mentioned in the description above? The one who loved with a covenant heart and mindset—died for those ardent ideals; he was brought back to life through his sacrifice to those ideals. He offered eternal salvation to any who had faith in him as ruler over the practice of those ideals. The only way those ideals continue to shape us today is through a very unique ongoing form of faith. Not just a faith in some unseen Superior, but a recognition that the Superior actually has a desire for continued interaction; has a passion for redemption of a corrupted world; is carrying out a covenant plan to de-marginalize the relationship with any who choose to share that faith…

> **—Loving that Superior with <u>all</u> their hearts and <u>all</u> their minds (All; none against the other)…**

> **—Loving their neighbors as themselves (all, none against the other)**

It can work. It does work. It's called *covenance*.

## IF SO, THEN

All that I've proposed is nothing but conjecture, unless internally tested. I can't prove any of it, unless I apply it and others see it working through me. So am I…

> **—Loving my Superior with all my heart and all my mind?**

> **—Loving my neighbor as myself?**

If so, then I should have a wonderfully dynamic relationship with said Superior. I might even converse with that Superior and might actually have a sense of direction that I firmly believe to be directed by that Superior. I might demonstrate a strange and uncharacteristic (as defined by humanity) covenant lifestyle based on my trust in the reality and authority of that Superior.

Does my life reflect the things I've been posing? I believe so, but if so, I now wonder why I'm dialoging with only you…and not also…with my Superior. After all, if the effort is with all my heart, and all my mind; then all of that should be offered, including my thoughts and voice, to my Superior. True that?

## IF SO, THEN

—Here we go: All others who have not yet thrown this book out the proverbial window are welcomed to walk along or away, but from here on, I am trusting in the power of my Superior to give identity and value to these words—to the benefit of all who are willing to risk their whole heart and mind.

*******

MY LORD AND SAVIOR, I should be humbly approaching you, should I not? I should be inviting the world to join yours and my conversation, experiencing the thrill and expectation that comes with a real-live *de-marginalized* spiritual encounter. And so I ask in confession: Do I take your gracious gift of covenance seriously enough? If we humans are serious, shouldn't we be striving to better understand and pursue the attributes of a covenant relationship with you—including entering into real-life conversation with you?

And there is the quandary Lord, that second principle which I tend to leave out of the equation, if I'm to take your gracious gift that seriously, I need to take your gracious commands as seriously, obeying them and passionately walking them out. That includes this very difficult one…the one as great as the first:

### *Love my neighbor as myself*

The words are so…troublesome. You are not, I'm sure of it, suggesting one of my neighbors or my favorite neighbors, but all my neighbors. And the neighborhood you speak of in scripture where I'm to love my neighbor is not just next door, not even just (certainly not excluding) beautiful Williamson County, Tennessee, but <u>all</u> neighborhoods in <u>all</u> corners of the world…where <u>all</u> your people dwell.

Lord, let me confess. There are neighbors I just don't like. There are people I do not trust. There are leaders and agitators and those not living up to my expectations that I want to convert into my image. And if I'm trying to make/shape others into <u>my</u> image; that means:

> ***I'm refusing to recognize the spiritual image you have provided me***

Which means…

> ***—I'm not faithful to my belief in you as God.***

These two covenant confessions of self-willfulness are so inextricably bound together; my mindset and my behavior so influenced by them: My Savior, how is it possible to overcome either or both acts of rebellion on my own? If I take your gracious gift of covenance seriously; if I'm serious, shouldn't I be striving to better understand and pursue the attributes of a covenant relationship with others—including entering into real-life conversation with them?

### IF I DO OR IF I DON'T

Lord, I know this is radical and strange, talking to you in the first person[55], but I'm really trying to understand the ramifications of covenance with you and others; how I can avoid marginalizing you and others.

### WAIT A MINUTE…

—Did I just suggest that you, God can be marginalized by me? Do I actually have that power? Perhaps it is the one and only power I do have and it is the one I want to relinquish most of all. I now believe, that by tying my love for you, the unseen Superior, to loving my very *seen* neighbor, a new challenge surfaces.

> ***How can I love someone who is unlike me?***

---

[55] As the <u>first</u> person?

Lord, for me this became a dangerous question to answer. I started by observing all those who seemed to me, just plain unlovable. They didn't think like me or do like me or believe like me. Some didn't care if I cared and some just didn't appear to care about…anything. So is that defining *Love* or is it better termed *Like*? We seem to have shallowed the deeper meaning of love in order to provide a convenient way to de-marginalize our global brothers and sisters. Are there many out there disagreeing with me right now? How would they answer the following?

> *If I'm living out the deeper principle of love—loving you, God; and also following through with the second—loving my neighbor as I love myself; then my neighbor will also see evidence of my unique relationship with you, my Superior.*

I know what happens when I respond to you in love, I've seen the extraordinary things you will do with that, but…forgive me; I have to ask, regarding what my neighbor witnesses—so what? I have experienced so many rejections: People who mock me, people who have faith in other things besides you, God; people who actually hate the idea of loving; people who are blind to hope of anything beyond their own self-sufficiency—narcissism, personal ambition or self-pity. I have opened my arms in hopes of relationship and have been seared by their burning pain. Maybe marginalization—me from them and them from me—is safest; is best.

But if that is the case, why have I found your love? After all, even the most despicable miscreant—though they may have buried the moment in the fathomless regions of their suffering—once longed also for the highest affection. We all have, I have; that fact cannot be marginalized. Or can it?

### Does a covenant lifestyle require belief in you?

I have found that some people I interact with want to avoid that question, when in fact; that investigation is the most exciting one of all to start with. That query begs another. One that no Atheist or distant Theist or Agnostic I have encountered dare ask:

### *"What does the Superior's superior-love look like?"*

97

Instead they (as I once did) want to ponder,

### *"If God does love, why doesn't he fix the world?"*

**WAIT A MINUTE…**

—Lord am I wrong to point this out? Are my very words marginalizing against others? Maybe I'd just better keep my perceptions focused on my own behavior, and let others read these convicting words through the filter of their own discerning hearts.

So, it's back to you and me, Lord. *Why do you, God, offer the blessing of a covenant relationship to me*? Am I deserving as Abraham was deserving? Or if I was to ask the more arrogant version of that question, *why would I be undeserving*? Would that be because, in my relationship with you I am discriminatory rather than inclusive. Do I dismiss you as inconvenient, unimportant or non-existent in some or all events of my life? What if I did try <u>completely</u> trusting in your existence as my Superior; not just including you as a convenient companion or a concept to be disputed or switched off like a light-switch when I'm done with you?

Oh the worst truth of all Lord: If you are the Superior, trust is not a factor at all. Why? God is God. If I don't trust you, it doesn't make you any less God. By nature, you are Superior regardless of my belief, and that can truth can tempt me to even more drastic rebellion. It may drive me further away from you and from anyone of my neighbors who don't provide for <u>my</u> <u>immediate</u> <u>needs</u>; who don't match up to my personal expectations.

That begs a question of you Lord, and one of my neighbors. Can I trust in the fact that you actually are concerned with me individually? Do I dare respond in kind? If so, it then circles back around to the way you ask me to behave toward others.

*Can I actually trust in the fact that you are truly concerned with the condition of other people, and the planet on which we all live together? Am I prepared to act out my love for others as you have acted toward to me, without expectation of an equal response?*

All and each of you could, and should ask the same question of me. You God, chose Israel, but then asked them to invite into spiritual relationship—through your example with the stiff-necked people of Abraham's lineage—all other nations and people.

> *"Love the sojourner, therefore, for you were sojourners in the land of Egypt.*
> *You shall fear the LORD your God. You shall serve him and hold fast to him,*
> *and by his name you shall swear."*    —Deuteronomy 10:19-20

Covenance was your original concept, Great YHWH. You called it your *plan*—designed with the intent that we humans walk together in agreement toward the discovery of a desired relationship, working toward new understanding...your understanding. Is it a stretch to think that we today should adhere to that same model—honoring the creation and the Creator?

I confess to doubts. For example, I have wondered if you, God, marginalize? Have you in your greater-good-planning set one group apart because you were pleased with or uncomfortable with their behaviors and spiritual orientation?

Actually, I know the answer to this question already because I'm part of the group who set up the conditions: Man, not God, marginalizes. *Lovingkindness* (including correction), *Steadfast Love, Long Suffering* are your efforts to allow time and opportunity to reset the error on our part.

**You, God, do not want a marginalized contract relationship with me, you invite covenant fellowship.**

Not only that, but you take your covenant relationship with me/us far more seriously than I do. How do I know this? Take the ongoing example of Abram. When you *cut covenant* with him, not only did you put him to sleep, thus assuming full responsibly for the covenant outcome, but reading on in the historical record, you continued to reveal your more complete intentions.

In Genesis chapter seventeen, I see of a whole new relational paradigm taking shape that would, and still does require the hard choice—whom do I choose to draw close to? God, and by example Abram, made his preference known through a covenant act, not to marginalize, but invite:

> *When Abram was ninety-nine years old the LORD appeared to Abram and said to him, "I am God Almighty walk before me, and be blameless, that I may make my Covenant between me and you, and may multiply you greatly."*
>
> *Then Abram fell on his face. And God said to him,*
>
> *"Behold, my Covenant is with you, and you shall be the father of a multitude of nations. No longer shall your name be called Abram, but your name shall be Abraham, for I have made you the father of a multitude of nations. I will make you exceedingly fruitful, and I will make you into nations, and kings shall come from you. And I will establish my Covenant between me and you and your offspring after you throughout their generations for an everlasting Covenant, to be God to you and to your offspring after you. And I will give to you and to your offspring after you the land of your sojournings, all the land of Canaan, for an everlasting possession, and I will be their God."*
>
> *And God said to Abraham, "As for you, you shall keep my Covenant, you and your offspring after you throughout their generations. This is my Covenant, which you shall keep, between me and you and your offspring after you: Every male among you shall be circumcised. You shall be circumcised in the flesh of your foreskins, and it shall be a sign of the Covenant between me and you."*
>
> —Gen 17:1-11

And the result for the rest of us, based on God's blessing to Abraham?

> *Now the point in what we are saying is this: we have such a high priest, one who is seated at the right hand of the throne of the Majesty in heaven, a minister in the holy places, in the true tent that the Lord set up, not man. For every high priest is appointed to offer gifts and sacrifices; thus it is necessary for this priest also to have something to offer. Now if he were on earth, he would not be a priest at all, since there are priests who offer gifts according to the law.*

> *They serve a copy and shadow of the heavenly things. For when Moses was about to erect the tent, he was instructed by God, saying, "See that you make everything according to the pattern that was shown you on the mountain." But as it is, Christ has obtained a ministry that is as much more excellent than the old as the Covenant he mediates is better, since it is enacted on better promises. For if that first Covenant had been faultless, there would have been no occasion to look for a second.*

> *For he finds fault with them when he says:*

>> *"Behold, the days are coming, declares the Lord,*
>> *when I will establish a New Covenant with the house of Israel*
>> *and with the house of Judah, not like the Covenant that I made with their fathers*
>> *on the day when I took them by the hand to bring them out of the land of Egypt.*

>> *For they did not continue in my Covenant, and so I showed no concern for them, declares the Lord.*

>> *For this is the Covenant that I will make with the house of Israel after those days, declares the Lord:*

>> *I will put my laws into their minds, and write them on their hearts, and I will be their God, and they shall be my people. And they shall not teach, each one his neighbor and each one his brother, saying, 'Know the Lord,' for they shall all know me, from the least of them to the greatest.*

>> *For I will be merciful toward their iniquities, and I will remember their sins no more."*

> *In speaking of a new Covenant, he makes the first one obsolete. And what is becoming obsolete and growing old is ready to vanish away.*

> —Hebrews 8:1-13

Now I believe I'm beginning to understand the difference between your desire and our desires more clearly, Lord. Our culture struggles with the covenantial concept as contracts seem to reward personal gain rather than common cause. It's little wonder that our modern-day concept of diversity also encourages traded; not common, benefits.

CHAPTER EIGHT—The Greatest Experiment

"Show me in Scripture:

The religion called Judaism
The religion called Christianity

There is no religion mentioned in the Bible, only relationship
God with people
People with God
Messiah with God and people

Life is not easier because of this
Relationship is a difficult thing—a *covenant* thing—an eternal thing."

—Mark A. Cornelius

MY GOD, YOU ARE A REVELATIONARY[56] DESIGNER. Even as you created…are creating…you want to tell us, reveal to us; expand the depths of us through your purpose with us. I love your desire to share. It is the very primacy of your true Final Solution.

I realize that not everyone is going to read the words above and be inspired in the same way. Some will say, "Oh no, Mark has turned socialist." Others might fear that I am invoking some kind of group-think-*kumbaya* event. Certainly "no," to the first, Lord; possibly "yes," to the second?

**COVENANT DE-MARGINALIZATION IN REAL-TIME**

From the beginning, you set in motion an integral model for society and individuals to work together, commit to one another. It involved a pledge of parties to adhere to a code of honor, seeking to walk/work toward a common goal—*Partners desiring the same purpose*. The parties exchanging assets and liabilities: sharing each other's belongings and burdens.

By example, you YHWH, taught early believers how important and vital such agreements— *covenants*—were in establishing profound, trustworthy relationships on which civilization could be nurtured and firmly founded. Great examples of how you, Father God, introduced us to the strength of covenant relationships with your partners; were Abraham, Moses and David. Even though they each had setbacks in honoring the covenant you established with or through them, they learned and became better followers by your correction and grace.

---

[56] Yes, I spelled that correctly.

What you are revealing to me through these historical examples is the failure of my own weak attempts to better the world. I have donated money; I've offered recycled clothes and goods; I have prayed within the safety of my sanctuary. But your story, your revelation suggests a very deviant approach to societal charitableness. To grasp the significance of your blueprint, I had to go back to an ancient definition: Your word for covenant suggests two possible meanings:

1. *Berith*; from the Hebrew *barah*—meaning to cut, a symbolic and or severing of old ways, bleeding together in mutual sacrifice.

2. The second opinion implies an Assyrian origin, *Beritu*—meaning to bind. Not unlike the first idea, it is an ironic word meaning joining two separate things to make them *one*.[57]

Whichever origin is accepted, Lord, I see your intention for us with you, and with one another—fellowship, not marginalization—and that means getting my hands dirty, entering into relationships with those who are sectarian to my way of life or who I may ordinarily desire to marginalize because of our differences.

One of those people, I have already confessed to depreciating is you, Lord Jesus. I can't speak for others—they will have to search their own hearts—but I have in fact marginalized you in your life's work and continue to marginalize your efforts to affect my life today. Why would I do that to the very one I profess to call King of kings?

Could it be that I don't recognize when I'm encountering or have the potential to encounter you? Could it be, not that you have disguised yourself, but that I have intentionally disguised you, to excuse my anti-social tendencies?

*I tell you I've not seen you hungry, thirsty, unfamiliar, without clothes, sick or imprisoned.*

*You tell me that whatever I've not done for one of the least, I have also not done for you.*[58]

---

[57] http://www.bible-researcher.com/ Covenant.html
[58] Gospel of Matthew 25:33-46

The dilemma is equally about my communal divorcing of you and the subsequent spiritual disunion. The quick thought is to nod my head in confession, exclaiming, "Yes, Lord, I chose whether or not to relate with you."—then drop to my knees in repentance. But based on that scripture I just referenced, what is the true repentance? Is it only to strive for a closer worship relationship with you? What about the subliminal message—your admonishment and conviction of me, not just to provide material goods to the needy, but to physically and spiritually commune with my fellow man?

### A RADICAL APPROACH

Whom to fellowship with? Whom to marginalize? Are those two questions really a right-thinking determination on my part? The very separation of the issues: fellowship and marginalization—betrays my doublemindedness. So if I reword the consideration and ask instead, "How do I invite all to fellowship?" If I reach out to others unlike me in a sincere desire for mutual understanding (not forced tolerance), and requested the same in return…an honest dialogue…what should I hope for?

### COVENANT FELLOWSHIP: A RISKY SOLUTION

*Tangibility*: a dangerous concept. If I draw near to others, hoping for a closer relationship with them and you Lord, I might experience the same ordeal that surfaced in my school dating days, that terrible phenomenon known across all cultures, called *rejection*.

That's the heart of it, isn't it? I fear that I either won't be acceptable to others, or more likely that they will tangibly react; verbally and even physically striking back against my offers of interaction and engagement in covenantial de-marginalization.

WAIT A MINUTE...

—Lord, I suspect you might counter my fears with a few spiritual questions to ponder:

*"Is the risk really that great?"*

*"Have I, your Lord, not given you strength and wisdom for such moments?"*

And the most uncomfortable question of all:

*"If I, your Lord, am God, is the risk you take on my behalf not worthy of your acts?"*

I'm sensing that you are suggesting I reconsider the more ancient paradigm for my day-to-day approach to life.

> You, God, have watched us reinvent your plan into our own idea of a mutually beneficial structure. With longsuffering, you patiently reminded throughout time of your fundamentally different approach – allowing individuals the free will to choose access to and inclusion in a new kingdom realm—with you as the Superior benevolent ruler of all; none deserving or receiving special status or rank; none to receive a better contract arrangement than the other.

> Mankind has fought against allowing your standard (individually and in community) since the beginning. Adam and Eve hid themselves from you, Jacob wrestled with you, Israel abandoned you, the nations tried to redefine you.

So who am I to be able to live out such an example? How do I attract others to live out your Covenant lifestyle with me? Where do we start?

**COVENANT FELLOWSHIP: "THE DAY-TO-DAY" OF A DE-MARGINALIZED SOCIETY.**

There is a very old word that people still occasionally throw around, and Lord, I'm not sure it's aboriginal meaning is now fully grasped. The term suggests that tangible element we were talking about earlier. Today we think of it as physical evidence, something that can be physically, clearly seen and/or touched; up front and personal; present tense. The word is *Manifest*. But Lord, there seems to be more to the definition. According to what I've read, Manifest is a verb. Instead of me observing a manifested object, I need to either be engaged in or affected by the manifesting. I need to be a part of the physical as well as the spiritual act of manifestation.

So what does that mean in plain English, Lord? Please help me understand how to manifest a tangible covenant relationship with others.

Again I'll meditate on a quote from Paul of Tarsus who suggests you, Lord, have already offered the solution by challenging us to be of the…*"same mind, having the same love, being in full agreement."* In other words, don't <u>contract</u> with one another; instead share the same vision…

—<u>covenant</u> with one another.

Great words, Lord, but I live in a marginalized world where people are encouraged not to be of the same mind and not to agree. Love today is defined as embracing individual rights and thoughts and struggling to make others understand my individual needs and wants. So the challenge is not just about how well I get along with you, or how well I get along with others; but in seeking commonality in a diversified world. I know there is a way, but it again requires adjustment. It starts with a thought that you once offered…

> "—Abide in me, and I in you. As the branch cannot bear fruit by itself, unless it abides in the vine, neither can you, unless you abide in me. I am the vine; you are the branches. Whoever abides in me and I in him, he it is that bears much fruit, for apart from me you can do nothing."[59]

—Beautiful love language, Jesus. You desire covenance and then you pray later, just before your self-sacrifice, that we should desire it as well…

---

[59] Gospel of John 15:4-5 ESV

"—I do not ask for these only, but also for those who will believe in me through their word, that they may all be one, just as you, Father, are in me, and I in you, that they also may be in us, so that the world may believe that you have sent me. The glory that you have given me I have given to them, that they may be one even as we are one, I in them and you in me, that they may become perfectly one, so that the world may know that you sent me and loved them even as you loved me."[60]

**THE PROBLEM**

But wait Lord, all this wonderful language depends on a belief system—a very specific belief system in fact. If that was not the case, I wouldn't have to be mentioning your name in this book because everyone else would have simply assumed I was calling out to Jesus. Since there is also clear evidence that some people reject you, I also have to recognize that there are those who take the rejection one step further, minimalizing the idea of a Supreme Being, outright dismissing you, YHWH as only a primitive notion. Some think you are nothing but a concept; at best a moral example only; at worst an archaic notion easily replaced by supposedly improved societal inventions. Now, as then, we have difficulty fitting you into the framework of our modern self-centric lives.

In fact then…

### —We live in a world of spiritual marginalization

And that, to me is the most frightening aspect of all, only because of where I have come from. As you know Lord, I was once one of those "dismissers", categorically refusing to acknowledge even the slightest chance that you exist.

---

[60] Gospel of John 17:20-23

Going back to Chapter One of history…and also Chapter One of this book, the origin issue that led to marginalization was a spiritual one.[61] We separated ourselves from you, Creator. In fact, many will read this and pose four different arguments from four distinct mindsets:

1.  "I don't believe in a creator, so how could I or anyone have separated from a superstitious belief?"
2.  Others will say, "I believe in God and we are fine with one another as long as he or she gives me what I want
3.  I believe in a Creator, but once created, we are left to our own devices to exist and succeed.
4.  I believe in God. He is God, I am not. What he has designed and inspired, I should be constantly pursuing, absorbing and living out.

Three of these statements marginalize any hope of an understanding of you, God. In fact, the people who believe the first statement are most likely at this point to marginalize this book and stop reading. I urge instead, pressing on just little farther because in understanding one another's mindset, we may each learn how to de-marginalize our world and our lives together.

WAIT A MINUTE…

—There might be people out there with yet another question:

*"Do you, God, marginalize us?"*

That is the twist to spiritual marginalization, isn't it, Lord? We accuse you of marginalizing us based on what appears to be some very empirical evidence. Namely, Genesis 3:22-24. But the driving-out/marginalization never appeared to be your intention. You had another plan that required others to join in rather than have benefits handed out in welfare fashion. You call it Redemption.

---

[61] No I didn't blatantly associate the word Spiritual with Marginalization in chapters One or Two. But you Lord, had to deal with Spiritual Marginalization early on. My context is inspired by your original context: Genesis 3.

There is an important factor I think I've picked up on here, God. Please offer your insight for validation. When something is redeemed, it is bought back for a price. You knew (because you are God!) that our human tendency would be to want something (relationship with you) for nothing.

You also knew that we humans seem to value something to a much higher degree if we have to strive for it. So, you planned far in advance to create a structure by which, in entering into a mutual agreement, you the Superior and we the lesser could coexist in a covenant (All for the same thing) environment. That agreement only required we acknowledge you and that is how you built a creative caveat into covenance:

> *If all I have to do is recognize your existence as my Superior to covenant with you, then it makes it very difficult to accuse you of marginalizing me.*

In turn,

> *If all I have to do is deny your existence as my Superior to denounce you, then it makes it very evident who is the true marginalizer.*

And that brings home the current dilemma:

> *How we have treated and continue to treat you, Creator, is the model for how we treat one another.*

God, you chose Israel, but then asked them to invite into spiritual relationship, the other nations, through your example with the stiff-necked people of Abraham's lineage. Is it a stretch to think that we today should embody that same approach? I know that religious organizations invite people into their buildings one day a week in hopes of establishing some kind of connection. But why aren't the "inviters" intentionally sharing their homes and lives the other six days of the week? Why aren't those same people seeking access to the neighborhoods and homes of the marginalized? Could they, like I, be worried about rejection or persecution?

You Lord, know this best of all: In a time when a master country of unparalleled influence popularized and encouraged strange, even perverse cultural norms. At a moment when

111

individuals and countries lost themselves and depreciated their deeper beliefs in hopes of not becoming targets of ridicule or mistreatment; in a land where your ways and your people were oppressed by an unwelcomed government determined to *overrule* you on the world stage—you appeared.

**MARGINALIZATION IN REAL-TIME**

> Your entry was not grand as I would have expected. Your humble approach in physical life seeming the polar opposite of what any might have imagined if God were to walk as a human. And how did we receive you? As a baby most did not recognize you, as a child you were ignored, as a man you were crucified. You joined the ranks of the marginalized.

"Oh," I might say now, "Had I been involved, I would have opened my arms to you, cherished and worshiped you, maybe even given you some friendly advice on how to work with us." Lord, I believe this denial of involvement through my own self-distancing from the events of your crucifixion is just another great example of how we humans justify our self-perceived nobility. "I wasn't there, how can you possibly accuse someone as good as me of marginalizing you in my heart and mind?"

**WAIT A MINUTE…**

—Was your sacrifice a form of marginalization? Here is the greatest paradox of all: You designed your New Covenant option—every nation, all for the same thing—to be completely inclusive, not exclusive whatsoever. Yet to those who have chosen not to join in, such an offer looks like one more example of marginalization—you God, punishing those who don't fall into line. How can such a dichotomy of perception exist? How is it, that one group can recognize your invitation as a perfect covenant invitation while the other group sees it as an imperfect contract?

**DE-MARGINALIZATION IN REAL-TIME**

> There are three men on crosses: Each has been marginalized by those in power and society. One of them had chosen long before his sentence to participate in the greater good designed by his Superior. The other two also had the choice of joining into covenant: One of them mocks and scorns the

one who predetermined his path. The mocker resented his plight and condemned everyone and anyone unlike him, regardless of their empathy toward him. In doing so, ironically he marginalized himself along with the rest of humanity.

The third man seeks relationship with the first. He readily confesses his offenses and asks for forgiveness, requesting covenant fellowship which is granted to him with true compassion, even in the midst of unbearable pain and eviction from most of the other onlookers.

Jesus, in studying this incredible event, I notice that the crowd seems unconcerned with the value of the ones on the cross, but instead are focused on the punishment. You on the other hand, seemed more concerned with those around you: To John and Mary; "Son, behold your mother, mother your son." To the criminal who honored you; "I tell you today you will be in paradise." To me and the rest of humanity; "Father forgive them for they know not what they do."

## WAIT A MINUTE…

—two different ways of reacting; one ordained as a higher achievement (whether people believe it Godly or not) and the other; the-same-old-thing mentality: Which do you, the hero of the story choose? How could this have happened? Why would you not act as others acted, what made you…makes you now…so unique?

You seemed unafraid to reveal yourself, even in your weak and bruised condition. And as God (my belief), you remained humble, in hopes of inviting just one more to be de-marginalized. Why can't I maintain that kind of love for others?

I can't judge the hearts and minds of others—how they see themselves reacting were they set into that sad moment. No-one knows the mind of another, except for you. No-one knows my mind better than me, except for you. Am I willing to admit that you might know me better than myself? Could that be another reason people try to marginalize you into non-existence—they don't want anyone else, especially you, God, knowing them better than they themselves?

Are we, society at large, now so entangled in conventional wisdom, that we cannot…will not consider the consequences if you indeed exist. As with culture being enamored with the chance that there is life on other planets, what if there is even an infinitesimal chance, those who believe in you are correct in their belief. If there is even a marginal likelihood that you are…God—shouldn't we be doing not just some things, but everything to investigate your presence? Shouldn't we; all of us, not just a marginalized few, be intentionally and intensively pursuing you and seeking a love relationship with you? I think to myself, *beyond my own belief in you, how can I break the cycle, how can I love you as you love us?* Your answer back to me is written for all eyes to see, and it is a difficult answer indeed.

"Love your neighbor as yourself."

So weird, how does loving others like me prove my love for you? Not that I can't or won't serve my community and the nations beyond. In our defense, Lord, over the centuries and into this era, the world, me included, has demonstrated some capability at stepping up to the plate to donate a dollar, offer support, lend a hand to build a better world. Even the Romans understood this.

Then again, even the psychopath thinks he is improving things by his actions.

We all know the fancy credos: Teach someone to fish and we will all be better. Lift up the downtrodden and we all improve. So we march out, even those who don't believe in you, to altruistically de-marginalize those who have been cast aside. What a good feeling it is to invite them back into the fold.
So, Lord, even in my concept of charity, my natural tendency is to contract rather than covenant with my fellow man—marginalizing those relationships and expecting them to blindly trust in my concept of your plan. Honestly, I try to do the same with you as well. But you correct me. It is not just the bodies and minds of others that I try to censure. It is their spirits that I try to regulate.

You long for each spirit, reminding me to forgive. "They know not what they do," you once said. And yet you seek to forgive each of us, even me, into relationship with you. If we will only ask, seek and knock for the same. Remember the statement in Chapter Six—Covenance is a LOT of work!—? That's why as Christians, we sometimes are prone to become invisible to not only our fellow humans, but more specifically to our brothers and sisters, because they…and our God might ask us to accomplish the un-accomplishable, sacrifice the un-sacrificable? No wonder the world of unbelievers looks at us with mistrust!

Your preference differs even from most who claim to be your devoted followers. You desire a path of complete covenantial unity, community, and commonality. Unity does not mean uniformity, community does not mean communism, commonality does not mean sacrifice of unique individual qualities that you engineered into each of us. So, Lord, I'm detecting a pattern here: There is a choice in life of:

**"I versus you", and "us versus them"**

Each suggests an opponent rather than a common cause. Is that our way and are we being intentional in our competition? What are we keeping from one another? What more can we be doing to be faithful to our covenant.

I, Lord, have prayerfully asked you to help me find evidence in the word and in example of the alternative to such an antagonistic approach and you have whispered the wisdom of Romans 12:3-5 into my heart.

> *"For by the grace given to me I say to everyone among you not to think of himself more highly than he ought to think, but to think with sober judgment, each according to the measure of faith that God has assigned. For as in one body we have many members, and the members do not all have the same function, so we, though many, are one body in Christ, and individually members one of another."*
> —Paul of Tarsus

Now that's meaty covenant language. I will encourage any who seek a better understanding of your desire for covenantial living, Lord God, to read the entire book of Romans. And I'll continue to pray for the fruit of those words to result in your true intention.

What is that intention, some will ask?

## CHAPTER NINE—Unity

*"And when they would be talking and Granma would say, "Do ye kin me, Wales?" and he would answer, "I kin ye," it meant, "I understand ye." To them, love and understanding was the same thing. Granma said you couldn't love something you didn't understand; nor could you love people, nor God, if you didn't understand the people and God. Granpa and Granma had an understanding, and so they had a love. Granma said the understanding run deeper as the years went by, and she reckined it would get beyond anything mortal folks could think upon or explain. And so they called it "kin."*

—Forrest Carter, The Education of Little Tree

LORD, I'VE BEEN TALKING A LOT, BUT AM I LISTENING AND RESPONDING ENOUGH? Is there a chance that I've been marginalizing our relationship by embracing all these heady concepts, but doing little—a marginal amount—to act them out? I see good people, doing good things and wonder; do they ever consider themselves *good-enough,* or worse, *better* than others around them? Is it possible that we present our acts of kindness, not as a testimony of your power in our lives, but as the concrete for our life's memorial stone?

I can't speak for others, I can only reflect on my own tendencies and I know that I've been guilty of *recognition-hunger*—the quest for approval from others. Forgive me Lord; I've even done things thinking I can gain your approval when…I am already approved.

Thanks for your grace in that and thanks for sharing your wisdom to inspire me in the right direction. Mine is not to invent good works, but to do the good works invented for me. But how do I know what those are?

As noted earlier, the words in the books of Deuteronomy 6, Leviticus 19, and Matthew 28 all have something to say—you to me—about that. But is there anything else I'm missing, any other message that you are trying to knock into my very hard head?

One seems to be trying to make itself more evident in my life, but I confess it to be a puzzling one:

> *And all who believed were together and had all things in common.*
> *And they were selling their possessions and belongings and distributing the*
> *proceeds to all, as any had need. And day by day, attending the temple together*
> *and breaking bread in their homes, they received their food with glad and*
> *generous hearts, praising God and having favor with all the people. And the Lord*
> *added to their number day by day those who were being saved.*

—The Acts of the Apostles, Chapter 2:44-47

**WAIT A MINUTE…**

—Am I suggesting to the non-believer that they must believe? Am I prodding believers to participate in some kind of proselyting; sacrificing by sharing their personal testimony of what they have received, in order to benefit to others? I know in my case, you, Lord convicted me to read this passage many times and helped me integrate it into the context of your complete message. There are reoccurring words in the text which suggest a very cohesive social structure.

## *All, Together, Common, They, Any*

Granted, the language is inclusive toward those who believe. That was (and I'm convicted to believe still is) the first order of business. But you have never been a God of only those who believe. You sent your son so that the world might be saved. How can that happen unless we offer our compassion as you did—when you walked the world—to those on the road that are walking a different direction?

Thank you for your humble example and your open arms, Lord, that I, and any marginalized journeyer willing to approach, may find a home of truth in the message of your good-will. I pray now in invitation, for others to respond. Let the dialogue begin!

> "Come to me, all who labor and are heavy laden, and I will give you rest. Take my yoke upon you, and learn from me, for I am gentle and lowly in heart, and you will find rest for your souls. For my yoke is easy, and my burden is light."
> —Matthew 11:28-30

**OPEN ARMS, THE MOST DIFFICULT SOLUTION**

Father God, you ask us to separate ourselves from the world, by entering into a relationship with you—the difference between this marginalization offer and all other separations, is that you have offered this redemptive familial inclusion to every single human-being who has ever walked the planet.

As a Christian, I claim honor in the idea that you offer holiness—separation of those who believe in your son as Savior—from those who do not. Your scripture even suggests a provocative title to our undeserved status. We are called *saints*—chosen ones—not by nature of our own efforts, but by the sacrifice of you, Lord Jesus.

So, you are teaching me once again what I thought I already knew:

*It's not just the physically or culturally aberrant that we sector off into convenient corners,*
*it is the spiritually marginalized—the very ones you encouraged us by your example, to touch.*

**UNITY VS DISUNITY IN COVENANT:**

Well that settles it then, doesn't it? I need to get busy seeking out covenant partners, inviting them to become part of the All: Inviting them to church and to think like me, to be like me and to worship like me…

—silly me, that's what I've already been doing, trying to remold your creation into my creation. It hasn't worked out well and the more I read your word, the more I see where you want something entirely different from a building full of people who all look and talk alike. Being likeminded does not mean dressing alike or even acting alike—you created us in you spiritual image, not in our designer-jean-desire-to-impress image. To the wounded traveler, the Samaritan did not look or behave as the righteous ones before him had looked and behaved. He first had to put aside his own bias and not fall prey to the social mores/notions of the day—after all, he was a Samaritan; a scourge to Jews of the day. He would have been expected to spit on the sufferer and pass on by, more so than any of the others who players in the story.

But he didn't. He was not a Contract Guy, he was a Covenant Guy. He was spiritually inspired toward a greater good for all, to be caring of another in need, as you God, care for all of us. Oh yes; and there is that other conveniently neglected observation:

*The Samaritan encountered and tended to the marginalized victim, not in church or through a government program, but on the road they both traveled in common.*

And that's the point isn't it? We should be reaching out, wherever we are, whatever the circumstances, to offer help and covenant reconciliation, regardless of the "other's" spiritual condition. They deserve your love reflected through me, as much as I deserve it, even at the risk that my efforts, however well intentioned, will be refused as repugnant.

**WAIT A MINUTE…**

—The realization has hit me: It isn't just "them" that are ill-defined and separated into exclusion from the big tent of social acceptance. If the broader definition of marginalized is claimed, then "We"—those, including me, who have been doing the defining—will also discover ourselves to be among the rank and file of the marginalized.

## SPIRITUAL INCLUSION—FOR THE LOVE OF "WE"

You Lord, GOD, have taught me how to include others in covenant. It starts with a simple expression of an inward thought…

### —*There is a problem…*

—And then a continuation with a purposeful paradigmic[62] shift…

### —*It doesn't matter whose problem it is, it's what we <u>do</u> about it.*

Whether we use the words contract or marginalization to define our problem, whether we de-marginalize our relationships with one another (You and me, me and them, we and you) by embracing covenants or treaties, there is only one option to eliminating the problem…

### —<u>*doing*</u> *it all together.*

And that is the challenge, isn't it Creator—not just <u>some</u> for the same thing, but <u>all</u> for the same thing? To keep peace, we must first define peace. That will result in a discovery: Until we all come to the same conclusion as to what defines peace, we actually will never achieve peace: Which is why the ancients never spoke (as we do) about keeping peace. They strived to <u>make</u> (actively create) Peace. Peace Makers stripped away the comforts of multiple truths that felt good for some; not all. Instead they sought one complete truth that did not marginalize the lives of one group to the advantage of another.
You knew long ago how this type of *Peace Making* would impact the world:

**"Blessed are the Peacemakers, for they shall be called Sons of God."[63]**

**"But I say to you, Love your enemies and pray for those who persecute you, so that you may be
sons of your Father who is in heaven. For he makes his sun rise on the evil and on the good,
and sends rain on the just and on the unjust."[64]**

---

[62] …made up word, but tell me it doesn't work in the context.
[63] —Gospel of Matthew, Chapter 5:9, ESV
[64] —Gospel of Matthew, Chapter 5:44-45 ESV

Am I Pollyannistic and naive in my thinking, Lord? Are <u>some</u> out there shaking their heads, thinking *this poor boy believes he's having a solutional[65] conversation with a real being outside of visible reality?* Could those "open-minded" types ever even dare try to imagine the potential of your reality and how that reality de-marginalizes every single one of us?

And from the other side, if I were to reach out with a peacemaking hand, would your redeeming sacrifice be diminished? Would your better way be risked?

Of course not, you assure me in your word. It is not only the *why* of redemption, but also the *how.* Sadly, our human history of *how* has not been stellar. Instead of listening for the opportunity, learning the personal biography of hurt that each of them carries, and then inviting your Spirit to heal, we unknowingly or uncaringly encourage a more divisive cycle, sifting and censuring the right from the wrong, the best from the worst, the privileged from the unwanted. Our churches and our institutions separate out those who don't quite fit our expectations; don't exactly match our theology or our social constructs. Not that we won't assist them, we just won't engage them on a deeper, more sacred level, becoming familiar with their personal creation story, daring to inquire of their salvation, whether or not they are even alert to the need for redemption, being bold enough if they say, "not interested" to hear the honest individual reply. And then compassionately following up with the most difficult question of all…

### *"—Why not?"*

**COMPLAINING IS ONE THING…**

What do I do? Where do we start? If "them" means all of us, I'd like to believe that everyone has a vested covenantial interest in forming a plan. But I'm not that naïve. I know that most folks, possibly even some of you reading this right now, don't think the problem is significant enough to de-marginalize their lifestyles. So, it's up to me and any of those folks, possibly even some of you reading this right now, to set a new example. It means purposefully reviewing our behavior to identify who it is that we are avoiding and ignoring. Who are we condemning and who have we shown unproven biased toward?

Earlier I suggested that you Lord, GOD, have taught me how to include others in covenant and that it starts with a simple expression of an inward thought…*there is a problem.* But you have also taught me that, to include others, I must not just think but see the thought

---

[65] See comment on footnote 45.

through. How? It starts with a simple expression which leads to an outward act. That expression..?

### —We have a solution

I'm challenged by your example, Lord, to *walk among them*. To ask an unfamiliar request of an unfamiliar person: "Tell me your Creation Story." Maybe it won't be that exact phrasing, maybe I'll just ask them to tell me about their origins. The hard part will be the next step. Shutting up and listening—really listening and learning who the speaker is. What might happen if I, and all of us, took 15 minutes of our day to seek out someone whom we don't know and…get to know them? God forbid; what if I did that with someone I think to be unattractive; poorer, less educated, religiously different, politically opposite, socially awkward? What if I abandoned my rhetoric and my opinions, instead patiently listening for an opportunity to learn who sits across the table: their needs, their pain; their hopes? What might the results of my sacrifice? How might my de-marginalized neighbors benefit? What might we become?

#### WAIT A MINUTE…

Is this the lesson-complete, Teacher? Or is there something more that I'm to receive? I confess that I have spiritually marginalized others…but can others acknowledge that they have denigrated my deeper values? Can we, every one of us, have the courage to admit that the spiritually marginalized are not just *them*…it is *us*? And what we have done to one another, we have then done to you.

Forgive us, for we still don't know what we are doing…without you.

Lord, I know that all of this is not just about listening, watching, and critiquing. It is about doing. That means some action on my part. I want to write about this and will dwell on the subject over a longer course of time. I desire to develop a more concise definition of what it means to be spiritually marginalized and how to de-marginalize. But beyond that, you are inspiring in me a new hunger to engage the disengaged, to offer a reliable sanctuary for those who feel they have had their voices muted, their beliefs squelched. I want to invite and openly share in a deeper discourse, where even the faith and practices of those who believe openly and bravely in you may be safely shared without condemnation or reprisal toward their convictions.

**PROOF**

There is a way to prove out the idea that you are a relational God waiting for us to de-marginalize you. That model suggests beginning a conversation with our Superior, just as suggested we do within our communities.

> *Listen to God's origins. How do you find out about the origins of an eternal being? ***side note: yes, if there indeed is a God, then God is eternal. How do I know? One way is by admitting the antithesis and rejecting its hold on me: If He is not eternal— then He is not God.*

**YOUR WARNING TO ME, GOD**

In offering comfort or encouragement to the needy, my efforts may very well be rejected. I might even be slandered and sullied for my exercise. And there will be some who simply self-marginalize, arguing points such as your purported invisibility, in order to avoid confronting you with their own inadequacies.

But how do I explain to others, my listening and responding to an invisible, eternal being who exists on a plain other than the physical one with which I am so familiar? How and where does one discover the origins of a non-created Creator?

**THE BOLDEST OF REALITIES**

I realize this is a Christ-believer's perspective, but I'd like to offer it anyway to anyone interested in working through the filter towards a possible truth…

> *—If John the Baptizer is correct in John 3:30: "He must increase, but I must decrease."*

And if…

> *— Paul of Tarsus is correct in Galatians 2:20: "I have been crucified with Christ. It is no longer I who live, but Christ who lives in me. And the life I now live in the flesh I live by faith in the Son of God, who loved me and gave himself for me."*

Then there can be only one conclusion;

**In our ending:** *There will only be God.*

## CHAPTER TEN—DOING

*"Do nothing out of selfish ambition or vain conceit. Rather, in humility value others above yourselves, not looking to your own interests but each of you to the interests of the others."* —Paul of Tarsus

I'M SURE THERE ARE OTHER REMINDERS of how I need to respond to your covenant message of inclusiveness. Right here in beautiful Williamson County, Tennessee, I'm reminded every day that others have less or more than I do. I can get very wrapped up in the comparisons; I can easily become envious of the "haves" while equally pitying the "have-nots". To me it's ironic, that many times, I'm not as concerned about economic differences—again: Williamson County (Hello, if there is someone impoverished; throw some cash their way!). My personal conviction, Lord, is to serve, as you direct, those who are victims of their social and spiritual environment. Drug addiction, child and sex trafficking, physical and psychological abuse, elitism; all of these diminish and marginalize our human condition.

## MARGINALIZATION IN REAL-TIME

Here's a painful reminder of how close and yet far away I am from serving as you served, Lord…

—My wife's job puts her in touch with a vast array of individuals whose beliefs and lifestyles vary widely. One such individual; I'll call him Bill, seemed worked with my bride on an occasional basis and shared his creation story with her. It was not a pretty experience. In short, Bills family; his parents, his siblings and all they touched were bitter and self-consumed. Bill himself struggled with depression, alcohol abuse, gender confusion and felt rejected at every turn.

Yet, he would call my wife and talk not just about his struggles, but his hopes. He had dreams of breaking through his pain, walking away from the world which told him he was worthless. My wife did her magnificent best to encourage him and speak Truth—God's desire for relationship—into this haunted man. And yet he kept acting out the same behaviors which brought him to his desperate point.

I met Bill too and found him engaging, friendly and willing to lend a hand when asked to work on a project. My relationship with him however was distant and superficial. There never seemed to be the time or the opportunity to engage in a deeper conversation. I thought to myself, *this one isn't mine to engage.* And truthfully, it didn't appear so. I thought my role was as a sounding board to my bride's experiences with Bill and to encourage her as she encouraged him. For the most part, the relationship between them rolled up and down challenging hills: Bill's parent both died, Bill went in and out of rehab programs, Bill was up and determined one day and down the next as he, his siblings and his other personal relationships battled one another. Yet there was hope as Bill still insisted he was preparing for a better pattern, a new way of life.

Then one day my wife got a call. Bill was found dead in his car in a vacant lot, the victim of an overdose. Whether by accident or intent, his journey in this life was over, the hope of it consumed by the darkness he dwelt in.

We don't know Bill's last thoughts. I don't know what brought him to that final sad point of marginalizing himself completely from those who might offer comfort to reignite his dreams. But my wife and I know that this was a soul worth pursuing, a soul worth engaging, inviting to the table of life's interaction and deeper quest for Truth.

So the loss, especially for my wife, but for both of us, is profound. What could be done, more than what was done? What word spoken or act taken might have influenced Bill to take another step in the direction of life rather than death? And Lord, then you spoke to me. Was it just about Bill? Or is it still about those surrounding him? Who is reaching out to his broken family and what friends he has to offer them the hope and the Truth that Bill struggled to comprehend and act on? It is not just a covenant with one that you seek, but a covenant with all. Those who knew Bill are still here; my wife and I included. Those who know others like Bill are still walking the streets of Beautiful Williamson County, Tennessee and the world beyond, minding their own business, trying to keep their lives straight and all the time missing the point that, to do so, we must all be earnestly trying to help the more marginalized among us to do the same. It starts with, but does not end with one person asking another, "Tell me your creation story." It continues with each and every single one of us more urgently pursuing that question, and its answers, together at the table of life's interactions and deeper quest for…you, Lord God.

What I've experienced with this and other life struggles, point to something higher than just a legal agreement. You are seeking relational unity of body, mind and spirit, not just between you and me, but including everyone.

Of course that takes a lot more work. You've already done the heavy lifting Lord, but that doesn't leave me off the hook. You ask me to respond by mimicking your behavior. By doing so I am not gaining points; I am only obeying—a very difficult behavior for me to live out consistently. After all, I have my own ideas on living in comfort and solitude. I deserve my freedoms and my hard-earned privileges…
don't I?

What if we are actually called to reach out to the Bills of the world? Are we humans being truthfully honest with ourselves, much less with you, if we refuse that profession? God

127

forbid, we might all come to believe we are somehow individually privileged to do whatever we want as long as we deem it good in our own eyes: As long as serving others serves us—Quid pro Quo.

## WAIT A MINUTE...

—Am I hearing you God, your voice of compassion; commanding me not to just create programs, not to just invest financially, not only to hold awareness seminars; but to seek out the same thing I should be seeking out with you...real, tangible meaningful, ongoing, longsuffering relationships with the marginalized? How do I step into their environment to meet and understand them; isn't that dangerous? Isn't that risky...to me?

Of course it's risky; what of value in life, isn't? The key is how to reduce the risk and increase the benefit?

## CREATION OF RELATIONSHIP

Lord, I can spout all day about being a good person and helping my fellow man, but how do I take that a step further? How do I live out the example and point others in the same direction without appearing preachy or self-righteous?

I ask only because I have experienced the negative from the other side of the fence; I too have looked down my nose at those who appeared to me sanctimonious when later I discovered they wanted nothing more than to help me, their neighbor. I too have to review with suspicion, my feeble motives toward the marginalized. My attempts to act nobly have been marginal at best: So I come to you in all humility, asking you, the True Expert, what is the eternal formula for establishing long-lasting covenance with another...with all others?

## DE-MARGINALIZATION IN REAL-TIME

There is at least one man out there who knows exactly how to engage in covenant relationship. I've met this humble soul and am amazed at his very simple approach. The one I speak of will enter a neighborhood and seek out the *strivers*—those in the community who appear to desire more in the way of life-changing benefits for those around them. That's right, he seeks out the "non-self-serving". That takes a degree of patient observation, but pays off when he then invites a deeper conversation. His invitation to each of these strivers...?

## *"—Tell me your Creation Story."*

What? That request assumes these strivers are somehow spiritual or at least religious in their outlook. Or does it? What this man discovered is that, even if people are not God pursuers, they are still easily able to frame their origins into a composition of life and seem eager in most cases to share their summarized experiences.

What also happens is that their tales inevitably reveal a theme: The ongoing search of a Greater Truth.

The man referenced above then offers to share his own experience in search for that same Greater Truth. In fairness, his conclusion is already found: *There is one Creator and He is the God of Israel.* But that discovery was one of intensive personal pursuit, driven by the kindness of a predecessor before him, inquiring the same…*tell me your creation story.* His sharing of creation begins long before his own existence. He shares about your conception and creation of the Garden, our fall, and your redemption plan, laid out through millennia of scripture.

He does not ask for a conviction or change of faith from others, just a dialogue. And that dialogue leads to so much more—an understanding common ground; not yet agreement, but a beginning of respect leading to a now shared quest for not just a truth, but The Truth.

Remarkably, this man (who shall remain unnamed for reasons about to be revealed) resides and seeks out these relationships in of all places, the Palestinian occupied territory of the West Bank of Israel!

Talk about risky, Lord. And yet, that man walks freely, boldly and respectfully among those whose fundamental beliefs appear converse to his own. Inspired by his example, I've tried, on a more minimal scale, to try his approach. Some people would think that such a technique would not be so difficult here in beautiful Williamson County, Tennessee where everyone gets along and everyone believes in the same things and every lawn is the same color green. But those people would be mistaken—remember Bill.
In my own exploration, you Lord, have revealed that the culture, economics, beliefs and identities here, are as widely diverse as anywhere on the planet—with individuals being just as protective and defensive of their personal belief and behavior bubbles as anywhere.

Amazingly, when I engage in the same manner as does my friend the creation-questioner—walls come tumbling down. So that now I not only am a more welcomed companion, but also someone to whom you have revealed an essential epiphany related and essential to the idea of a greater good…

### —*A Greater Good requires a Greater Truth to exist*

Well that begs a question now, doesn't it, Lord? A question from all of us to you: *Isn't truth…truth? What could possibly be a Greater Truth?*

I've researched the question a great deal on my own, and it seems that many writers, poets and prophets have had a lot to say on the subject. Several of my favorite examples are quoted:

> *Teach me your way, O LORD, that I may walk in your truth; unite my heart to fear your name.*
>
> —David of Bethlehem

> *I am the way, the truth and the life.* —Jesus of Nazareth

> *Men occasionally stumble over the truth, but most of them pick themselves up and hurry off as if nothing had happened.* —Indirect citation from Sir Winston Churchill[66]

**WAIT A MINUTE…**

—What in the name of marginalization is wrong with doing what I think is good for me? Am I to deny my own wellbeing at the expense of other's needs? Each individual reading this book, I'm sure is replaying their own historical examples in their minds of how they have been marginalized and of how they have marginalized others.

But equally it seems there are many examples of someone sacrificing their own comfort, recognizing their own needs to be insignificant to that of their covenant partners. Personal examples are unnecessary, Lord. History is replete with such tales.

---

[66] https://quoteinvestigator.com/2012/05/26/stumble-over-truth/

The greatest and truest tale of all is yours. You invented and implemented the first covenant. You fed us covenant language and tangible covenant examples to teach us the ultimate lesson...

—You love and desire relationship with me and with every individual, so much so that you marginalized yourself, becoming human to embrace humanity...

—You have asked, and continue to ask me and every individual to help grow that relationship, for, and with you, sacrificing our individual good, for the greater good.

**WAIT A MINUTE...**

—It's not that simple, is it? Oh no, de-marginalizing isn't just about "chumming-up" with others; you have convicted me about that. If it were so, then all that money and lecturing and all the political rhetoric we have broadcast would have fixed the world long ago.

**A TRUTH LEADING TO THE GREATER TRUTH?**

All of our efforts are supposed to be conjoining—not just giving resources, but becoming people engaged with strangers, until they are not strangers...until we are not strangers. But how do I start that process? What must I do to become...available for those kin as well and I'll need to keep my eyes and ears open for them, responding rather than just acknowledging their import.

And then there is the follow up. That's where we all, particularly me, appear to fall short. The new popular aphorism, based on an ancient Chinese prover, has become:

*"Give a man a fish and he is fed for a day. Teach a man to fish and he is fed for life."*

Good words those. But even this wisdom leaves out a greater instruction of yours, Lord. I found it in the book of Matthew, the 28th chapter:

*"Go therefore and make disciples of all nations, baptizing them in[a] the name of the Father and of the Son and of the Holy Spirit, teaching them to observe all*

*that I have commanded you. And behold, I am with you always, to the end of the age."*

If I'm actually following those instructions, I have to be doing more than an initial *net-casting seminar* with my fellow humans. I need to be going out in the boat and we must fish together. We must examine one another's techniques in order to improve both.

That's not to say that I should be looking for people to fish with, who are better at fishing than I, unless I sense a need to up my game. You encourage that, but you command me to go out and find others who are struggling with their daily fishing exercise and you tell me to teach them <u>all</u> that you have taught me. That is not a one day or week long endeavor. That takes an extended commitment and it also doesn't mean spouting off a lot of rhetoric. It means showing them who I am, who you have changed me to become. It means being vulnerable about my own struggles and giving a real tangible helping hand to someone who has caught a barracuda and is trying to wrestle it into the boat.

It's time to live out what I claim to be all about— covenant relationship. No marginalization will be encouraged, unless it is to separate out any spirit of hostility and unwillingness. Now is the moment for what has been called for from the beginning…

**THE COVENANT FELLOWSHIP BEGINS**

—Lord, I'd like to introduce you to your people. People, I'd like to introduce you to your God.

**MY FINAL WAIT A MINUTE…**

—How absurd: First, how dare I assume that I have the ability or the right to make such acquaintances. Second, haven't you, God, already made yourself known? Haven't your people, all people planet-wide had ample opportunity to respond or to reject? Why would I need to jump into the middle of that fray? But you Lord, have asked all of us to love the deeper, greater love that you have been encouraging us to recognize for thousands of years. Haven't at least <u>some</u> of your people been trying to right the wrongs of oppression, dispel human power-plays and reject marginalized injustice on a personal level throughout the generations? But are <u>some</u> enough?

Who am I to ask such questions? I'm just a player, marginalized like any of you other people. All I want is to stop acting out my own rebellion that distances me from others, and from my God. All I desire is to share the amazing covenant relationship that has found me. Does that give me any right to ask the same of you…does it matter whether I have such a right? Maybe; surely it is right without any need of our consent. Maybe it is a greater good without need of my or anybody else's permission.

Lord, I spoke briefly of my own rebellion in Chapter Eight, but if all I talk about is how I avoided you, never sharing with others how you did NOT avoid me, but instead confronted and wooed me, then there would be no true north to this book.

People, I've confessed my efforts to avoid encounters with many of you, wanting little or nothing to do with many even in my neighborhood and local communities, much less those who profess different lifestyles and beliefs. Are you prepared, as I am preparing to explore the greater good and discover the greater Truth alongside of me?

If so, then let me be as vulnerable with you as possible. It's time for me to share my creation story with you, inviting the same in trade. Yes this is a turnaround of sorts. I'm sharing first—authors are like that. But your opportunity to share will come, there is no doubt. It is how we approach one another, not when that is crucial.

**COVENANT DE-MARGINALIZATION IN REAL-TIME**

This will be a little different in that I will be sharing a confession to you, my God, and simultaneously a testimony to you people still reading along. So here is my creation story:
I did not grow up in poverty, at least not the economic version. As a matter of fact, but North American standards, our family was smack dab in the middle of middle-class. By the world's standards, we were wealthy. I was the third of three children, all baby-boomers who grew up hearing and witnessing the evolution of our parents as depression era kids into post-WWII achievers. My father traveled for his sales profession, leaving my mother—a very intelligent women who might have run a company or served in some high profile capacity—to raise us kids. When my dad was present and on behalf of my mom, I'll say they did an amazing job of encouraging our curiosities and teaching us the social graces. To their credit, I observed from a later point of view, they tried hard to help us become unique individuals, and one of the tools they used was *the question.* I don't mean by this a singular question, but we were instilled with the boldness to question everything. All things; including the existence of you, God.

In the culture of the times, people might go to church occasionally as a social pronouncement (*We look good doing this*) and I learned from my folks early on how to pose for society. There was much more going on behind the scenes that we didn't want others to know about. My father's strained relationship with his mother—a severe puritan-woman who had once been a circuit preacher. There was the stress of my own mother's roll in the family which trapped her in a lifestyle, causing her to succumb to depression and ultimately to her prescription drug abuse.

Still we put on a good front. I was not the most popular kid, as a matter of fact, in summary; I was the runt. Picked-on and bullied I found my own ways to cope including reading just about anything. By my early teens, my author-heroes included Voltaire, Sartre, James Joyce, Walt Wittman and a wide array of other celebrated humanists.

I convinced myself of my own importance and concluded quickly, with my mentors to back me up, that you, God were nothing but a notion, a mythical method of man used to control humankind.

And then in high school things changed radically. I actually made real friends. I actually appeared to matter to others outside my immediate family. More so, one of my new friends invited me to play guitar in a band. Did I mention that music was the pulse of my existence? Of course you knew that, God and in a quirk of your designed plan, I was lured into, of all places, a church; a place I had only visited on Easter Sunday (and that had been many years prior)! The band was one of those early 70's Jesus groups and after my first visit, I was convinced they were quite insane.

That was when a very, VERY unusual thought entered my mind. *I'll show them!* Odd, what was it I was going to show them? The only arsenal I had with which to combat their warped views were my humanist pillars. They would not be willing to listen to me espouse my superior ideas; another tact was called for. I needed to disprove their crazy theology. I needed to demonstrate just how much nonsense guided their lives.

And that's how you snagged me. In order to debate them, I needed to know them. I needed to learn their teachings in order to pick them apart. I sat through a confirmation class in which I questioned everything; doubted all; suggested countless alternative realities. But in the truest reality, the one question I failed to ask myself was the one you had been whispering into my ear all along. *Why do I care about these people and their beliefs?*

In the end was my beginning. One night I looked up at the stars and saw the vastness of what I didn't know. I realized that no matter how much I wanted to think humankind had well-explained our origins and our reason for existence; in truth no-one, not one, not even Buddha, Mohammed, or any of my existential buddies had achieved or even come close to perfection. In fact, perfection existed already and chose to reveal itself rather than prove itself. You, Jesus sacrificed yourself out of a love I could not (and still cannot) explain. Why would you, a perfect being die to vanquish all of humankind's sin? Why would you ask for a relationship with the imperfect? Why accept those who rejected…marginalized you? There and then I learned humility, and it was not my own. It was yours. By your love, I then became nothing, to be reborn into your creation.


I could go on. There are many more spiritual nuances to my journey, especially in my early years—events I had no idea would affect my beliefs, fed from a source I had no idea existed. It is now so evident looking back that I can't deny your hand in my life, Lord. Not that I am anything special. I think all of us, if we are willing to take off our blinders will see your maneuverings. You do not to force faith, but offer exploration. If any readers want to know more about my particular experiences, contact me and I'll be glad to share. For the purpose of this book however, the story is not about me. It is about how the opportunity for each of us to come together with all the rest of us is made readily available by the Creator of covenant relationship. Bottom line:


### *Marginalization is totally unnecessary*


Much of this story, I've shared openly before. But what I have minimalized in the past is how creative I have been at trying to redesign your plan, God; to become my plan for myself and all those around me. Though I have shared with my God, my family and my fellow man, I have only done a marginal job of entering into covenant conversation, all inclusive. What I mean is that, yes, I can easily share my thoughts in a religious setting such as a worship service. And I can do pretty good job of relating in a social or work setting with others. But am I able to honestly reach out to those around me, learning of their own struggles and victories, encouraging not only dialogue, but a true effort to help those in need; celebrating with those who are striving to overcome? Of all the questions this one I can answer honestly. No, I can do nothing on my own. Which begs the greatest question of all: Who can do a worthy thing to the benefit of humankind? The answer to that question is the greatest of all replies…

## —*Only you, Lord.*

Regardless of my own struggles and victories, questions, and answers; mine is not the most interesting story of faith. The most interesting story of faith is that of you, my fellow marginalized neighbors. Maybe you have concluded something far different than I have. Maybe your journey has been rougher or smoother. Maybe you've never questioned anything deeper than what you plan to do for the day. Maybe you are asking why you should even continue one day longer.

I can't answer your questions for you, but I can walk the path of discovery with you. I can't change your life, but I can show you the miracle of change in my own and point you to its orchestrator. Maybe that's not of any interest to you at all, but if it is…what might be the result of such a deeper relationship with the rest of us; and with God?

I would love to pursue that de-marginalized covenant path, by your side.

# EPILOGUE

*Let brotherly love continue. Do not neglect to show hospitality to strangers, for thereby some have entertained angels unawares. Remember those who are in prison, as though in prison with them, and those who are mistreated, since you also are in the body. Let marriage be held in honor among all, and let the marriage bed be undefiled, for God will judge the sexually immoral and adulterous. Keep your life free from love of money, and be content with what you have, for he has said, "I will never leave you nor forsake you." So we can confidently say,*

> *"The Lord is my helper; I will not fear;*
> *what can man do to me?"*

—Hebrews 13:1-6

**A SPIRITUALLY DE-MARGINALIZED WORLD—PICTURE THAT!**

Paradise: a non-existent place? Yet we can describe it. We have opinions about it. We even write books about and fashion beautiful art depicting it. How can a fictitious place consume so much of our collective imagination? After all, paradise is not just my idea, not just yours. Every single person on the planet has a notion about it. Eden, Utopia, Nirvana, Shangri-La, and Elysium, along with many descriptive adjectives: bliss, shalom.

I also recognize a place that I would like to think is paradise, but is not: Beautiful Williamson County, Tennessee; for though it is a lovely landscape rich with human interaction and vitality, it is too a community which has marginalized elements of society in order to personify a way of life that is unlikely to be duplicated on a global level. Yet even B.W.C.T. can strive for the paradisiacal high ground, as all communities still might.

To do so, we must fine tune that definition. What is the essence of paradise, or using the name of names, the *topper* of the list: Heaven? And why is there such a deep-seeded desire to define such a place? Why do even atheists and those who want nothing to do with the concept of an afterlife, hold fast to the hope that a perfect state of being can and should be pursued?

My own position is pretty obviously projected throughout this book, but taking that away for a moment, there is a commonality somehow wired into us. It encourages, even drives most to pursue a better, higher purpose and existence. In this book I have called it, *the greater good*. Regardless of mine or any other's beliefs, one thing is certain. There is only one thing that keeps us from achieving personal and societal perfection. There is only one barrier to discovering how and where paradise dwells.

Although some of you may not believe as I do about a certain individual who lived in the first century of the Common Era, Most would agree that he had some pretty remarkable things to say about paradise. Depending on the text you refer to, it was also called the Kingdom of Heaven, or more problematically, the Kingdom of God. But to me, Jesus of Nazareth's most remarkable comment about the subject was made as he hung in agony on a Roman cross, brutalized and marginalized by most all who had praised his approach to life. At that moment, he turned to a criminal on the cross next to him and said, "Truly, I say to you, today you will be with me in paradise."

This is seen as one of the most controversial passages in the Bible. The man Jesus spoke to had not professed him to be Savior. He had only recognized an obvious point: Jesus did not deserve what was happening to him, while the criminal himself surely did. I won't pretend to know the complete answer as to why this last-minute defending-man verses the other on the cross who mocked my Lord, was invited into paradise. The theological complexities of that moment alone might become another book. I will suggest that no matter what else is said about you, Jesus, you are the perfect reader of hearts.

Ask the women at the well; ask the many plagued with disease. Ask the demon possessed man on the cliffs of the Decapolis; ask Peter upon his denial. Ask me. You, Lord, know what hides behind our feeble words and actions. You know who and who not desires the fuller life. You, Jesus were always seeking a covenant, treaty with those around you. You were always joining marginalized hands, one to another with those who would reach out to you with their own hands and hearts.

So whether or not one believes in a Savior, achieving paradise requires what Jesus offered: Forget yourself, die to yourself; be reborn by following his example. What was that example?

***Do to others as you would have them do to you. Even to your enemy. Even to God.***

Can we join together in such a covenant as that? Will you join me in the pursuit? I'm willing to begin by stripping away my pre-conceived notions and concerns about you. Can you de-marginalize your thoughts about me? Can that place called paradise…the Kingdom of Heaven, exist between us…within us?

**—This is not The End**

*Stay where you are. Find your own Calcutta. Find the sick, the suffering, and the lonely right there where you are — in your own homes and in your own families, in your workplaces and in your schools. You can find Calcutta all over the world, if you have the eyes to see. Everywhere, wherever you go, you find people who are unwanted, unloved, uncared for, just rejected by society — completely forgotten, completely left alone.*

—Mother Teresa

## Author - Mark A. Cornelius

Mark A. Cornelius has authored numerous books, musicals, video productions, and a journal ministry.

His works include *Believement—Breaking Through the Belief Barrier, RUT Management—Discovering Adventure in the Routine of Life, Thunder Buffalo Goes Home, Welfare Christianity,* and the popular fiction trilogy, *The Ruach Saga* including *The Singularity, Seconds,* and *Bronzeman.* Mark's most recent work is titled *Marginalized.* All of Mark's books are available at www.RUTmanagement.com.

Mark has authored other insights and blogs, all of which can be obtained on his website: www.MarkCornelius.me.

**You can experience my passion for writing at www.MarkCorneli.us.**

**Travel with me at my blog www.DeepEndFaith.blogspot.com. E-mail: markc91754@comcast.net**

**Facebook: www.Facebook.com/v4641singularity.**

Thanks for the journey together!

## Illustrations: Shay Nicole Cavender

Shay Nicole Cavender is a native of Nashville
Tennessee. She began expressing an interest in art
at an early age. She takes particular interest in
drawing and creating animals and fantasy creatures.
Shay majored in Graphic Design at the University
of Tennessee at Martin to develop her unique style.
She continues to hone her skills, working as a
graphic design consultant and freelance
artist/designer.

Made in the USA
Columbia, SC
11 April 2019